# Dorothea Johnson's

# ENTERTAINING And ETIQUETTE

For Linda

Merry Christmas from Pat
and my warmest wishes,

Dorothea Johnson
December 82

# Dorothea Johnson's

# ENTERTAINING
# And ETIQUETTE

Published by **ACROPOLIS BOOKS Ltd.** ● Washington D.C. 20009

**ACROPOLIS BOOKS LTD.**
Colortone Building, 2400 17th St., N.W.
Washington, D.C. 20009

Printed in the United States of America by
**COLORTONE PRESS, Creative Graphics Inc.**
Washington, D.C. 20009


**ACROPOLIS BOOKS**
are distributed in

**EUROPE AND THE BRITISH COMMONWEALTH**
by Paul Maitland, 2/16 Mount Sion,
Tunbridge Wells, Kent TN1 1UF, England

**JAPAN**
by Atlantic Book Service, 23-17 Akabane Kita,
3-Chome Kita-Ku, Tokyo 15

**PAKISTAN**
by SASI Ltd., State Life Bldg #5
Zaibunnisa Street, GPO 779, Karachi 3

**ELSEWHERE IN ASIA**
by ICTO PTE Ltd., Wing On Life Bldg.,
150 Cecil Street, Singapore 1


**second edition**


Library of Congress Cataloging in Publication Data

Johnson, Dorothea,
    Entertaining and etiquette for today.

    Includes index.
    1.  Etiquette.  I.  Title.
BJ1853.J63                    395           79-960
ISBN 0-87491-241-5

# To
My husband Les
and my family—Bebe, Liv,
Ann, Ted, Julia and Tom

No book is ever the product of one person. I am grateful to those who helped me, especially Barbara Ann Morris, who kept my "writer's juices" flowing. Robert Hickey, a talented designer, made many superb suggestions that were readily accepted. The work and support of Sandy Trupp, Kate Bandos, Sandra Alpert, and Nancy Stewart are greatly appreciated, and to Al Hackl who believed in me—my gratitude.

And then, of course, there are the many women and men who attended my classes, read my columns, and supplied me with dozens of questions that are within these pages.

Above all, thanks to Lois Dean, whose editing and typing produced everything ahead of schedule.

To my many other friends, who in one way or another made this book possible: *Thank you.*

Dorothea Johnson

# Contents

# Foreword

This is not a definitive book on entertaining or etiquette, nor is it meant to be. But I believe it will give confidence to the most inexperienced party-giver and party-goer and give reassurance to those who need to be reassured that what they've been doing is right.

There should be no mystique about entertaining or etiquette. The rules are simple—enjoyment of people, kindness, and consideration.

This book is about Entertaining and Etiquette—for *today's* more relaxed lifestyles.

Why such a book? Aren't there standard books on etiquette and dozens of books on entertaining?

Of course, there are hundreds of books available. But I think there is a need for a helpful up-to-date book for *today's* party-givers and party-goers. I hope that I can help you maintain a high standard of entertaining, however modest or elaborate your endeavors, help you refresh your talents, and reinforce your feelings about etiquette. After all, etiquette

13

isn't dead, it has simply undergone some changes. Many of these changes are for the better and certainly are in keeping with our more informal lifestyles.

Today, gourmet foods, fine wines, liquors, or a stately mansion are not requirements for entertaining. Nor does one have to consult a heavy volume on etiquette to be assured of doing the right thing. There are no absolute rules about parties today and the best rule to remember concerning manners is *do unto others as you would have them do unto you.* After all, the purpose of manners is not to make an impression, but to show consideration for others.

Dorothea Johnson

# Introductions Titles & Names

# *Introductions*

**Q.** *I get confused when I introduce people. I'm never sure who is introduced to whom. What are the rules?*

**A.** Hard and fast rules for introductions exist today only in business, the military, and the diplomatic corps. The person of lesser importance is introduced *to* the person of greater importance, regardless of sex: Mr. Greater Importance, Mr. Lesser Importance.

With equality among the sexes, the old rule that *a man is always introduced to a woman* is antiquated. However, common sense tells us to introduce a thirty-year-old man *to* a seventy-year-old woman, even though he holds a high level office or has impressive achievements. On the other hand, a twenty-year-old girl is introduced *to* a fifty-year-old man.

*The person being introduced, regardless of sex, is mentioned last.* To introduce two people in a group where everyone is on a first-name basis, just say, "John Jones, Mary Smith." If you know only one of two people by his or her first name, then include the Ms., Mrs., or Mr. for both, to be consistent. For example: "Mr. Jones, Mr. Smith."

If you are introducing a number of people, it's easy. Mention the new person's name and then give the names of the others in the group. If you can't remember all their names, it is acceptable and practical to suggest that they introduce themselves. Don't use expressions such as *shake hands with* or *make the acquaintance of.*

Don't tack on *my friend* to one of the names when introducing two people. It implies that the other person is not a friend. A man should never say *meet the missus* or *meet the wife.* If you are introducing relatives, clarify their relationship to you. "My brother, Tom Smith." "My mother, Mrs. Smith," or "My mother, Helen Smith."

It is always correct to introduce yourself to whomever you do not know at a social function. The fact that you both are guests is sufficient. This applies to business functions, too.

**Q.** *When introducing my husband at a social gathering I never know if I should introduce him as Mr. Robertson or John Robertson. He doesn't know how to introduce me either. What is correct?*

**A.** Never refer to your husband or wife as Mr. Robertson or Mrs. Robertson in social introductions. If the people know your last name, all you need say is, "John, my husband," or "Mary, my wife."

**Q.** *Today, many businesswomen are retaining their maiden names. How does one introduce a husband and wife with different names?*

**A.** Introduce them as Mary Jones and her husband, Bob Smith.

**Q.** *How do I introduce Mary Smith and Bob Doe who are living together but are not married?*

**A.** Introduce them as Mary Smith and Bob Doe. It's not necessary to comment on their living arrangement.

**Q.** *I was always told to wait to be introduced at parties, but at large cocktail parties no one bothers to introduce my husband and me. Shouldn't the host or hostess introduce us to all of their other guests?*

**A.** It is impossible to be personally introduced to everyone at a large party. Usually guests are greeted at the door by the host or hostess and introduced to the other guests in the immediate area. Introduce yourself! Don't wait for your host or hostess—they have their hands full.

**Q.** *Does a woman rise to be introduced when new people enter the room?*

**A.** Yes. A woman should stand for any introduction. The old rule of a woman rising *only* to greet a prominent person, someone elderly, or a member of the clergy is no longer valid, thank heaven. Today, everyone in the immediate area rises to greet a newcomer, regardless of their sex

# Titles

**Q.** *My husband is a doctor and I've always introduced him socially as "Dr. Doe." A new friend tells me I am incorrect. Have I been wrong all these years?*

**A.** Yes. In social introductions, neither spouse refers to the other in the third person, as "Dr. Doe," "Mr. Doe," or "Mrs. Doe." If the people know your last name, all you need say is, "John, my husband," or "Mary, my wife." If the woman has become well known by her professional name, she should be sure to mention her married name when introducing her husband. "Mrs. Jones, I'd like you to meet my husband, John Doe."

Refer to your husband (or wife) by his (or her) given name when talking socially to either women or men, even though they may be younger. "John will be arriving later." If you wish to be more formal, you may say, "my husband" (or "my wife"). To employees, clerks in stores, etc., refer to your spouse as "Dr. Doe," "Mr. Doe," or "Mrs. Doe."

# Addressing the President

**Q.** *My husband and I went to a state dinner at the White House several months ago. There was a receiving line and as we passed by it shaking hands with everyone, we called the President "Mr. (last name)." I was later told by another guest that we were wrong, that I should only call him "Mr. President." My husband and I are still upset over this incident which put such a damper on an evening we expected to recall with warmth and happiness. What is the correct way to speak to the President of our country?*

**A.** Mr. President or Sir is correct. His name is never used at any time when addressing the President. You should not have let this *faux pas* spoil your evening. Stop brooding, it's in the past! In the future, do your homework.

# Unusual Last Name

**Q.** *I have an unusual last name which is often mispronounced. Am I rude to correct people?*

**A.** No. By all means do so.

# Invitations
# & Other
# Correspondence

Written invitations
Reminders
Thank You notes
Business correspondence
Telephone invitations
Verbal invitations
General invitations
Christmas cards

Dorothea Johnson

# Written Invitations

**Q.** *My husband and I received an invitation by mail to a party. Shouldn't we have been told the type of party so we could plan accordingly?*

**A.** Yes. It's totally unfair to guests to receive this type of invitation. Invitations, written or oral, should be explicit as to the kind of party: dinner, cocktail buffet, etc. Also include date, hour, place, and by whom given. It is a courtesy for the hostess to indicate how she and her husband will be dressed.

**Q.** *When writing an invitation on plain folded notepaper, should I use the front sheet or the inside sheet?*

**A.** Use the front sheet.

**Q.** *What is meant when* Regrets only *is on an invitation?*

**A.** You are being told to notify your host or hostess if you cannot accept the invitation. *Regrets only* is totally impersonal, in my opinion. It tells me that the hosts are figuring on a certain number of guests and they don't care who comes.

**Q.** *I am planning a luncheon for twenty-two women. May I write* luncheon *on my invitations or should I put* buffet luncheon *since it will not be a luncheon which is served at the table?*

**A.** *Buffet luncheon* tells your guest exactly what to expect.

25

**Q.** *How do I address an invitation to a married couple when the woman has retained her maiden name?*

**A.** Husband's and wife's names, although different, occupy one line. It doesn't matter whose name is first.

Mrs. Alice Jones and Mr. Robert Cox
Street Address
City, State, and Zip Code

**Q.** *What is the proper definition of the initials R.s.v.p., on an invitation?*

**A.** R.s.v.p. is the abbreviation for *Répondez s'il vous plait,* meaning *please reply.*

**Q.** *We received a party invitation with a smaller card included that reads as follows:*

*Mr. and Mrs. _____ will attend*
*Number of guests _____*

*Does this mean we are allowed as many guests as we wish and to fill in the number? The outer envelope was addressed to Mr. and Mrs. John Doe.*

**A.** No. The invitation was extended to the people whose names were on the outer envelope.

# Reminders

**Q.** *In December we were invited to dinner in a private home by telephone. Later we received a reminder and map in the mail. Invitation was written in the lower left-hand corner of the envelope. I thought the reminder and map were very thoughtful; however, I've never seen* Invitation *written on an envelope before. Is it correct and what is its purpose?*

**A.** Yes, it's correct and just as thoughtful as the reminder and map. Its purpose is to let the recipient know that he or she is receiving an invitation and not a greeting card. Many people get busy during the holidays and neglect to open their mail daily.

Mr. and Mrs. Lester Edwin Johnson

Buffet supper
Saturday, September 20th
7:30
7913 Deepwell Drive
Fairfax

To remind                          (over)

---

Mary,
    We are looking forward to
seeing you and tom again.
    There will be (14) of us.
    Les will be wearing a dark
business suit and I shall wear
a midi-length evening dress.
                    Warmest,
                    Dorothea

Wednesday

reward. Somehow, even though she could see what fun you had, hearing from you later makes her feel good. Whether you had the time of your life or just a pleasant evening, thanking is polite. After all, you were a chosen guest.

**Q.** *After a dinner party I always write our host and hostess a thank you note. A friend tells me I am wrong, that the note should be addressed only to the hostess. Is she correct?*

**A.** Yes. Correctly, a thank you note is addressed to the woman of the house as is the salutation. However, always mention your host in the note. If he prepared the dinner, make a special note of this in your thanks. Home entertaining today is often a joint effort and both participants' contributions should be applauded.

**Q.** *My husband and I gave a buffet supper for his office staff. Out of thirty-seven people who came, one woman telephoned me to say thanks. Is it no longer considered good manners to call or write a note of thanks to one's hostess after a dinner party?*

**A.** Yes, it's still considered good manners to write a note or telephone your hostess within a few days to express thanks. The ones who don't are inconsiderate, ignorant, or just plain lazy.

**Q.** *When I write my hostess a thank you note do I sign with a joint signature such as Mary and Bill?*

**A.** No. Even if your note expresses the joint thanks of a couple, the note should be signed with only one signature.

**Q.** *When are joint signatures suitable?*

**A.** For greeting cards, mailgrams, postcards, or on a card that accompanies a present.

**Q.** *I just attended a very elegant cocktail buffet to celebrate an anniversary. Many of the guests and I brought gifts. Should I write my hostess a thank you note or can I consider my gift sufficient? Also, should she write me a thank you note for my gift?*

**A.** I think a short thank you note from you would be in order—or a telephone call. The hostess should also write you a note or call and thank you for your thoughtful gift.

# Business Correspondence

**Q.** *Often I receive a business letter signed "Mary Doe". How do I address the envelope and the salutation when replying? Ms., Miss, or Mrs.?*

**A.** Ms., when there is no indication of the writer's preference.

# Telephone Invitations

**Q.** *Sometimes when I telephone and invite guests to dinner they will not give me a definite yes or no and I'm left* *hanging. When they finally respond with a no it's too late to ask another couple. When can I do in the future about undecided guests?*

**A.** Tell the undecided guest that you need an answer within twenty-four hours for planning purposes. If you do not hear from "undecided" within that period of time you should call and get a definite yes or no.

**Q.** *I am very disturbed about people's indifferent attitude about responding to written invitations. Often I don't know how many guests are coming. Is there a solution?*

**A.** Yes. Telephone your invitations. You will get an immediate yes or no. If a guest isn't sure he or she can attend, say that you will call back the following day for an answer. Often one can't rely on a call being returned. Make sure you tell those you invite pertinent details—type of party, date, hour, place, and also include what you and your husband will be wearing. About five days before your party, send a reminder.

# Verbal Invitations

**Q.** *What can I do when my husband issues a verbal invitation to a couple I have not met? They work with him and he speaks of them often.*

**A.** The invitation should be followed up and repeated by you.

**Q.** *My husband received an invitation for both of us. He forgot to tell me and we missed the party, which caused us some embarrassment. How does a man handle these verbal invitations?*

**A.** When your husband receives an invitation for you both, he should say something such as, "I'll have Mary call you about this." This is a courtesy to the wife and it prevents confusion in the matter of invitations. A couple should always apprise each other, in advance, of joint social obligations.

**Q.** *I was talking to a friend at a luncheon when a neighbor joined us. The neighbor invited my friend to her house for coffee and practically ignored me. I felt embarrassed and my friend acted very uncomfortable. Can you comment on invitations delivered in person?*

**A.** Extend oral invitations in private. Don't invite Anne in the presence of Barbara if Barbara is not invited also. Even if you plan to invite Barbara it may appear as if she's an afterthought and was asked only because she happened to be standing there.

**Q.** *A few weeks ago I ran into a friend in the grocery store. We chatted and she invited my husband and me to dinner. I completely forgot the date, now she is furious with me. It's awkward for the recipient of this type of invitation; yet, I don't know whom to blame in this case. Can you enlighten me?*

**A.** The hostess is at fault. Invitations should not be issued when chatting with a friend in the grocery store. She may forget details before jotting them on her calendar. A hostess who issues this off-hand type of invitation should always follow it up with a telephone call or written invitation.

Dorothea Johnson

# General Invitations

**Q.** *How far in advance should I invite guests for a dinner party?*

**A.** Invitations, either oral or written, should be extended about three weeks in advance. For special occasions, such as a Christmas party, four weeks is proper. If the urge strikes you to throw an impromptu party, be sure the guests don't feel they are last minute fill-ins. You might say, "Tom Smith just arrived unexpectedly and I was hoping he'd have a chance to meet you. Tomorrow evening at seven?"

**Q.** *How can I get people to reply promptly to my invitations?*

**A.** Telephone your invitation instead of mailing. State clearly who you are, the type of party, date, hour, and place. If your invitation is accepted, tell the guest what you and your husband will be wearing. This is a kindness and prevents confusion in the matter of dress, as it varies throughout the country. Five to seven days before your party, mail a reminder.

**Q.** *If I have declined an invitation for my husband and me to attend a dinner party and later find we can go, may I call the hostess to tell her we've had a change in plans and are free on the date of her party?*

**A.** No. I am sure the hostess asked another couple as soon as you declined. You cannot put her on the spot by your change of plans.

**Q.** *Recently the wife of a couple who had declined my dinner invitation called the day before the party to say their plans had been cancelled and they would love to come after all. I said no, but felt uncomfortable. Did I do the right thing?*

**A.** You have two choices. You can say no, that, in effect, you have filled the seats, or you can let the guests come and perhaps change from a seated dinner to a more informal buffet supper. You might set up another table and invite more guests. This is a personal matter and one should use one's own judgement.

**Q.** *We spend a great deal of time trying to find homes to which we have been invited. Many new areas are not on the maps yet; hence, our constant lateness. Is there a solution?*

**A.** Whether one lives in the suburbs or the city, it is a kindness to send new guests a map or directions. Your guests will be grateful and you will be delighted to see them arrive on time without any difficulty.

**Q.** *Would you please clarify the following invitations for me:* Cocktails, Cocktail buffet, Buffet, *and* Dinner. *I am confused. What time is best for each party?*

**A.** *Cocktails* means drinks and simple hors d'oeuvres or appetizers such as nuts, dips, and chips. A cocktail party can be scheduled from 5:00 to 7:00 P.M. or 6:30 to 8:30 P.M.

*Cocktail buffet* promises the guests that they won't go home hungry. Drinks, roast beef or ham, meatballs, pâtés, cheeses, finger-type desserts, and coffee are served. It's still a stand up and eat affair and is scheduled from 6:30 to 8:30 or 7:00 to 9:00 P.M. Often small plates are provided.

*Buffet* is a dinner but denotes the manner in which it will be served. Guests serve themselves. The usual dinner hour would be correct, anywhere from 6:30 to 8:00 P.M.

*Dinner* is a seated affair where food will be served by your host, hostess, or a servant. The time could be 6:30 to 8:00 P.M.; for a formal dinner, 8:00 P.M. Keep in mind the times mentioned are flexible. They are usually determined by your locale or the habits of you and your guests.

Q. *Why can't hostesses be more explicit with their invitations? We were invited to play bridge one evening last week and the hostess said, "Don't eat, we are serving food." Food was dessert and coffee. Do you have a solution?*

A. Everyone should make their invitations crystal clear. Guests like to know what to expect. Therefore, after telephoning an invitation and stating the type of party, date, hour, and place it's to be given, I always send a reminder stating one of the following:

Cocktails

Cocktail buffet

Dinner

Buffet brunch, Buffet luncheon, or Buffet supper

Luncheon and bridge or Dessert and bridge

Dinner and bridge or Bridge and dessert

Q. *I hesitate to use the French R.s.v.p. on invitations these days. Obviously, many people who are not socially aware do not know what these initials means. Is there a simpler way of getting people to reply instead of telephoning them?*

A. I would like to see these antiquated initials done away with entirely and use one of the following on written invitations: *Please reply* or *Please respond*. They mean the same as *R.s.v.p.* but are more contemporary.

**Q.** *I received an invitation to a dinner party. In the lower right hand corner* semi-formal *was written. I've never seen this before. Is it correct?*

**A.** No. Dress is either *formal* or *informal*, and today we are seeing *casual* more and more.

# Christmas Cards

**Q.** *How can I prune my Christmas card list?*

**A.** Go over your list and omit names of persons with whom no meaningful relationship exists. Don't complain about a long list, simply think matter-of-factly that you are sending cards only to out-of-town friends and relatives, but plan to extend local greetings by telephone or in person.

**Q.** *When signing a personal Christmas card, whose name is signed first?*

**A.** When cards are signed, the person signing usually puts his or her name last. When husband and wife have cards imprinted, the wife's name is first. A personal Christmas card should always include a written message. This goes for any greeting card.

**Q.** *Must I send a greeting card to everyone who sends me one?*

**A.** No. If you see someone from whom you have received a card, thank the person and add something personal about the card. If you don't see them, a brief phone call will suffice. Out of town cards with written messages should always be acknowledged. It's not necessary to rush a card in the mail the day before Christmas. After the holidays write a thank you note on a New Year's card, personal note paper, or any other colorful holiday notepaper.

**Q.** *How does one correctly address a Christmas card to a family that consists of a couple and two children?*

**A.** When addressing the envelope, write *Mr. and Mrs. John Doe.* Don't add *and family*, but include the message for the family inside the card.

**Q.** *Each Christmas I receive dozens of beautiful cards which I put in the trash after the holidays. They are so lovely I would love to recycle them. Do you have any suggestions?*

**A.** More and more economy-minded people are cutting up their old cards and using them the following year as nametags for gifts. Take a regular card and cut it smaller, using as much of the picture as possible, and then cut around the edges with pinking shears. Use a paper hole punch and make a hole to put the ribbon through. The solid color part of a card that doesn't have writing on it makes a nice tag also. Any card, birthday, etc., can be recycled this way.

There may be groups in your community that would be delighted to use your cards for making tree decorations, decoupage, and other projects.

# Today's Living

Eating out
Compliment
Confidence
Lecture
Uninvited guests
Pet etiquette
Children
Telephone
Houseguests
Engagements
Shower
Wedding
Anniversaries

Dressing for the occasion
What to wear?
Drinking
Guest etiquette
Guest duties
Guest bathrooms
Gifts
Gifts of food
Flowers
New acquaintances
Friends from other countries
Living abroad

# Eating Out

**Q.** *Our kitchen is going to be completely remodeled so we will be eating out in restaurants a lot. Who goes first and who sits where? My husband and I need some pointers.*

**A.** If there's a headwaiter, waiter, or hostess to guide you to your seats, the woman goes first. Otherwise, the man leads the way, chooses a table, and seats the woman, usually on his right or across from him. The woman generally is given the seat with the best view or the one out of the way of passing traffic. In restaurants with banquettes, the woman is usually seated on the banquette. When two couples are seated together, the women sit on the banquette.

# Compliment

**Q.** *I find it hard to accept a compliment without going into a long dialogue. What do I say?*

**A.** When you are complimented, the only response necessary is, "Thank you." Don't disparage yourself. If someone admires your dress, don't say, "This old thing, I got it at a bargain basement sale." A simple thank you is sufficient.

# Confidence

Q. *I have not done a lot of socializing and, therefore, I get very nervous when I know we are going to a party and will meet new people. Because of my husband's new job we will be invited out a lot and I know we will eventually have to entertain in our home. What is wrong with me? Can you give me some tips on how to be poised and confident?*

A. Lack of confidence is probably our most natural enemy. To overcome this problem we should expose ourselves to new people and new ideas. Experience and learning are the best confidence builders. Courses in make-up, grooming, cooking, entertaining, and flower arranging are all helpful. Many local schools offer courses in human relations that are designed to help people with problems such as yours.

# Lecture

Q. *Recently I have been attending a number of art lectures. The chattering of some people in the audience makes it impossible for me to hear the speaker. They visit, talk about their children and houses—in general, everything but listen to the speaker. Would you please comment in the hope the guilty ones will recognize themselves and not ruin these worthwhile lectures by talking.*

**A.** I will comment but I doubt that it will do any good since obviously they don't go to hear the speaker but to hear themselves. It is the height of rudeness to converse during a lecture. I hope you offenders get this message and don't run interference for the speaker's dialogue. Save your witticisms, clichés, and gossip for later.

# Uninvited Guests

**Q.** *Last night an uninvited neighbor rang our doorbell just as we were about to sit down to dinner. One of the children let her in and she saw the food on the table, yet she stayed and chatted for thirty minutes. Needless to say, our food was cold and had to be reheated. I didn't really know what to say or do. How does one handle a situation like this?*

**A.** If an uninvited guest drops in as you are about to sit down to a meal, it is certainly proper to excuse yourself and ask the caller to wait for you in the living room. After dinner, you could ask her to join you for coffee. It is a good idea to instruct your children on family rules about phone calls as well as callers during dinner.

**Q.** *What can I do about friends who just drop in without calling? Often I am not prepared to see guests, but I open the door anyway.*

**A.** You don't need to open the door unless you want to. Let your friends know you would like a call before they drop in.

# Pet Etiquette

**Q.** *A few days ago I spent an uncomfortable hour at a friend's house trying to drink a cup of tea while her dog licked, drooled, and jumped on me. "He adores you," cooed my hostess. Needless to say I didn't adore him nor the visit. What about dog etiquette?*

**A.** Etiquette begins with the person, not the dog. Dog owners should never assume that their friends share their love and devotion for Fido—this goes for all pets.

**Q.** *A couple I met last summer called to tell me they would be driving through this area on a trip. I invited them to spend the night with me. They arrived with a large dog that stayed near them every place they went in my house.. Shouldn't I have been told about this dog so I could have made arrangements for him at a nearby kennel?*

**A.** Yes, you should have been told about the dog. Anyone who has an animal should always tell the host or hostess in whose home they have been invited to stay. It's up to the hosts to indicate if they want the animal to stay in their house or tell the guests they will make arrangements at a local kennel. Guests should not assume that their animal is included in any invitation.

# Children

Q. *At some parties we attend the family pet or baby is often the center of attention. Either the pet or the baby is crawling on my lap and I simply can't relax. Please comment.*

A. At the start of a party it's fine to bring in a baby to be admired. The same applies to young children. Older children can learn party behavior by being around at the start of your party but should not be asked to spend the whole evening. Some people are afraid of dogs, allergic to cats, or horrified by hamsters, and white mice. This advice about babies, children, and pets applies only to parties, not to family gatherings or the night when a couple of close friends come to dinner.

Q. *With the new relaxed etiquette, should I teach my young children to stand when an adult enters the room?*

A. Yes. Children stand when introduced to an adult or when an adult enters the room. They remain standing until the adult is seated.

Q. *We recently invited two couples to dinner. One couple showed up with their six-month old child. We were not prepared to entertain a young child. The evening was totally child-dominated. How could anyone assume a child is included in an invitation when this was never discussed?*

A. Invited guests should not assume their child is included in an invitation. If a hostess is apprehensive about a couple bringing children, be specific and tell them it's an adults only evening.

Q. *My husband and I want to do some entertaining but we hesitate because we have two children under five years of age and a dog. What do you recommend?*

A. Keep your menu simple, serve food that needs little or no last minute care. Get a sitter for the children so you can enjoy your guests. Pets are best kept away from the party area.

Q. *We were invited to a dinner party where two small children were serving drinks and appetizers. A glass was dropped by one and I was splashed with ice and scotch. The child burst into tears but his mother said, "Any adult could have the same accident." Still crying he brought me another drink. Do you think small children should be used as servants at dinners that are not family affairs?*

A. No. Small children do not belong at an adult party and certainly should not be used to serve drinks. If an eight year old has social aplomb, he can help to show guests where to put their coats or perhaps pass nuts, but not drinks. Children should not be asked to recite poetry or sing for guests who aren't members of the family. Babies can be carried around by a parent for a quick view by guests.

Dorothea Johnson

# *Telephone*

**Q.** *I have always answered the telephone at home by saying, "Mrs. Smith," or "Smith residence." A new acquaintance tells me I'm wrong. Am I?*

**A.** Yes. "Hello" is the correct way to answer a home telephone in this country. Only a servant should say, "the Smith residence." "Mrs. Smith speaking," may be revealing too much, considering the crank callers, salesman, and pollsters who work by telephone.

**Q.** *What can I say to a friend who constantly calls me on the telephone just as I sit down to dinner with my family?*

**A.** Immediately establish the fact that you cannot talk and will call her back when it's convenient.

## *Telephone Tips*

Since the telephone is such an important part of our lives, good manners should be an integral part of our telephone behavior and conversation. Here are some helpful hints and telephone tips.

The area near the telephone should always have a light and be equipped with paper and pencil for quick jottings.

A guest who must use a telephone should be led to the bedroom extension, if there is one, so that the call can be made in private and not inhibit other guests' conversations. The call should be as short as possible.

If a guest must make a long-distance call, the caller should charge the call to his or her own home or office telephone number. This service can be accomplished by contacting the operator. The host or hostess is spared the embarrassment of collecting money from a guest.

Don't allow a small child, no matter how cute or clever, to answer the telephone. Your caller may never get the message through to you.

Don't ask a child to tell a caller you are not in, when in fact you are. This teaches a child to lie. If you are unable to talk, have the child say, "My mother is unable to talk at this time. Could you please call her back or would you like to leave your name and telephone number?"

A child should *never* ask, "Who is calling?"

A child should not be allowed to yell a person's name to summon him or her to the telephone. Instruct the child to go directly to the person and tell him he has a phone call. This applies to all ages.

If the caller asks for a person who isn't in at the time, ask if you can take a message. Then, make sure the person gets the message.

Americans hold the world record for talking on the telephone. There are more than 154 million telephones in the country and approximately six calls per telephone are made each day. Our statistics are provided by a representative of the C&P Telephone Company of Virginia, a subsidiary company of the American Telephone and Telegraph Company. See the front pages of your telephone directory for a Consumer Telephone Guide and call your local telephone company business office for another helpful guidebook on telephoning.

# Houseguests

Q. *We recently moved to the east coast. I arrived before my husband and rented a house that I couldn't move into for a month. During this time I stayed with friends. I used their car and made some long distance telephone calls. I offered to pay them when I left, but they said no. I feel obligated to repay them for the extra expenses they incurred. How can I handle this?*

A. Make an estimate of the telephone calls, and the gasoline you used when driving their car. Send a check for more than that amount with a note of thanks. As soon as you are settled in your new home, invite them to dinner.

# Engagements

Q. *My husband and I have been invited to an engagement party. Do we take a gift and is another gift expected when the couple marry?*

A. A small gift is sufficient for an engagement party since you will probably want to give a wedding gift too. Consider one large gift for both occasions.

Q. *I was engaged to my college sweetheart for over a year. A week before our scheduled wedding he backed out. Must I return the shower and wedding gifts?*

A. Yes.

# Shower

**Q.** *My sister is engaged to be married. Since no one has offered to give her a shower I want to, but I've been told I shouldn't. Why?*

**A.** Showers for the bride-to-be are given by friends, not relatives.

# Wedding

**Q.** *I am a widow who plans to marry a widower. We each have a grown son from the first marriage. Could my son give me away and could his son be his best man?*

**A.** Yes.

**Q.** *I am a widow who plans to marry again and my fiance would like me to wear a white wedding gown. Would it be proper for me to do so?*

**A.** Off-white would be suitable, but not a pure white dress. Any of the pastel colors are fine for a second marriage.

# Anniversaries

**Q.** *My husband and I will be celebrating our twentieth wedding anniversary in June and we are planning a large party at our country club. The gift for a twentieth anniversary is china. I would like to select a china pattern so if guests desire they may purchase a piece for me. I am not a new bride, but could I register my pattern at the department stores?*

**A.** The custom of selecting a china pattern and registering with a store is for an engaged or newly married woman—not for one celebrating her twentieth anniversary. If you want new china you should purchase it and not put yourself in the position of a new bride.

# Dressing for the Occasion

Invitations that specify a certain type of dress may confuse newcomers to an area. Remember these definitions when dressing for the occasion, but keep in mind that there is considerable variation around the world. If in doubt ask your hostess.

*White tie.*
    Full evening dress. Rarely worn today except at official White House functions and embassy parties, by the father

and escorts of debutantes, and at formal weddings. Must be worn to any affair when the invitation reads "White tie." The woman wears her prettiest, dressiest long dress. There is a corresponding uniform for each of the military services.

*Black tie.*

A man wears a dinner jacket (tuxedo) or the equivalent military uniform. The woman can wear the same dress she would wear to a white tie occasion. Evening pants or a midi-length evening dress also are suitable. Black tie should not be worn before 6:00 P.M.

*Informal.*

Just a cut under black tie. A man wears a business suit and tie, or the equivalent military uniform. Never a leisure suit or sports coat. For evening functions, a woman wears a long skirt, long dress, midi-length dress or the dressy pants designed for evening wear. If the invitation is for late afternoon, a woman would wear a dressy daytime dress.

*Casual.*

A man wears a sports coat, with or without a tie, depending on the casualness of the occasion; a leisure suit; or slacks, shirt, or turtleneck. A woman wears slacks or a casual skirt, long or short. For a patio barbeque on a warm day, shorts are suitable for the man or woman.

Dorothea Johnson

# What to Wear?

*Q. My husband was transferred to the east coast a few months ago from the southwest. We had been here only a few weeks when we received an invitation by mail to attend a cocktail buffet given by my husband's boss and his wife. In the lower left-hand corner was R.s.v.p. and a telephone number. I called immediately to say we would love to accept. In the lower right-hand corner was written* informal. *We went to the party dressed as we expected everyone else to be dressed. My husband wore a turtleneck sweater, no coat, plaid trousers, and I wore a pantsuit. We were shocked to see the hostess in a long, dressy dress and the host in a dark business suit and tie. All the other guests were dressed like the host and hostess. We felt very uncomfortable and only stayed about thirty minutes. It's confusing! We felt we were informally dressed and they formally dressed. I refuse to go out again until I know for sure how to dress. What does informal mean on the east coast?*

**A.** Informal is just a cut below black tie. The other guests, your host and hostess were correctly dressed. You and your husband dressed in a casual manner. Perhaps acceptable, when the invitation reads informal, in certain parts of the country but not the east coast. If in doubt always check with your hostess. The thoughtful, kind hostess tells her guests what to wear, or she tells the guests what she and her husband will wear, i.e., "My husband is wearing a suit and tie and I am wearing a long hostess dress or a midi-length evening dress."

**Q.** *What about the couples who show up at parties looking like the "odd couple?" Often the woman wears a long, dressy dress and jewelry while the man wears a denim or suede leisure suit with his bare hairy chest exposed. Or the man will wear a dark business suit and tie while the woman wears daytime casual clothes. Can't these couples get together on their outfits?*

**A.** I think there is a lack of communication between these "odd couples." Any couples, married or single, who are considerate of each other will see that their outfits are coordinated. A caring couple will pay special attention to each other in this matter as in most other matters. The rest simply don't care.

**Q.** *We are planning a dinner party. I want to tell my guests to dress up but I don't want to sound dictatorial. What can I say when I telephone my invitations?*

**A.** When inviting guests, be explicit as to what to wear for the evening. An over or under-dressed guest will feel out of place. Simply say, "Tom is wearing a dark business suit and tie, and I am wearing a midi-length evening dress."

**Q.** *I feel like serving my guests a hot dog when they show up at my elegant dinner parties dressed in casual daytime clothes. How can I tactfully let them know I expect them to dress up?*

**A.** Tell your guests what to wear or tell them what you and your husband will be wearing.

**Q.** *My hands tend to be cold and damp. May I wear gloves at a cocktail party?*

A. No. Gloves should always be removed when eating or drinking. Remove both gloves, not just one. Spray the hands with antiperspirant to eliminate damp hands.

Q. *I have been married for three weeks to a military officer. We were walking down the street and I asked him to carry my umbrella which he refused to do. His only excuse was that he wasn't supposed to. Why?*

A. An officer wearing his uniform does not carry an umbrella. It's simply not part of the uniform.

Q. *I never know where to put my evening bag and gloves when we go to someone's house for dinner. May I place them on the coffee table during cocktails and next to my plate when we have dinner?*

A. No. Do not clutter your hostess' coffee table with your bag and gloves, and never place your bag and gloves on the dinner table. Keep them in your lap or find a table out of the way that isn't being used and place them on it. A large daytime handbag is discreetly placed on the floor next to one's chair.

Q. *Is it appropriate to wear a long dress to a daytime event, say a 2 P.M. wedding, or a retirement ceremony followed by a reception?*

A. Very few rules exist in fashion today, but one that seems to hold fast is that long dresses should not be worn before 5 P.M.

# *Drinking*

**Q.** *At our dinner parties my husband and I excuse ourselves to put the food on the table. While we are out of the
room our guests pour fresh drinks which are wasted
because about this time we announce dinner and wine is
always served. Can you offer a solution?*

**A.** Yes, try my method. One of you should always be with
your guests. My husband remains with our guests. I handle
the final food preparation, allowing twenty to thirty minutes.
When I go to the kitchen my husband announces quietly,
"Last call for drinks." This eliminates wasted drinks and
prevents guests from trying to take their glasses to the
table.

**Q.** *Recently I was a guest at a large cocktail party where
another male guest drank too much. I was trying to be
friendly and helpful and offered to follow behind him in
my car to see that he reached home safely. The hostess
acted very annoyed with me and said, "He is our responsibility and is not to drive his car any place." I thought
each guest was responsible for himself. Who is responsible
when a guest drinks too much at my house?*

**A.** You are responsible. That's what it means to be a host.
If a guest drinks too much, see that he gets home safely,
but don't let him drive. Send him home with friends or in
a taxi. He will thank you later.

**Q.** *I don't drink. Alcoholic drinks just don't appeal to my
taste buds. Yet I'm often teased and even told a drink is*

*good for me. Many times I've taken a drink to prevent all this, then I just hold the drink in my hand. Please say something about the host who feels it's his duty to ply every guest with alcohol.*

**A.** When someone says, "No thanks," to alcoholic drinks, the thoughtful host or hostess will offer soft drinks or fruit juices. We should all beware of the host, ensconced in the comfort of his own home, who pushes drinks on his guests in the name of hospitality. This isn't hospitality—it's rudeness.

**Q.** *I don't drink but I would like to order a non-alcoholic drink without attracting attention. Can you suggest some non-alcoholic drinks?*

**A.** *Bloodless Mary* (also called a Bloody Awful): tomato juice, no vodka, dash of worchestershire and tabasco.

*Nellie Collins*: Gin-less Tom Collins

*Wyatt Earp*: Lots of ice, half and half mixture of orange and pineapple juice—or any fruit juice and ginger ale.

As well as juices and soda, Perrier water is also a popular drink.

**Q.** *I am a widow who recently met a widower. We are both in our early sixties and enjoy each other very much, but I am bothered by the following: He comes twice a week for dinner and each time brings a bottle of wine. We never drink a full bottle but he takes the remainder home with him. This habit bothers me. Is he cheap?*

**A.** Yes, and also tacky to take home an opened bottle of wine.

Dorothea Johnson

# *Guest Etiquette*

Q. *When I enter the room at a party, whom do I greet first?*

A. The hostess and the host, then the guests.

Q. *Sometimes we have guests who will not leave after a party. What polite steps can I take to let them know the party is over?*

A. Do not keep refilling glasses. Begin making post-party motions—emptying ashtrays, collecting glasses. Mention that you have an early appointment. If this doesn't work, now is the time to speak up and say that it was great fun, but unfortunately the party is over. Stand up and slowly start toward the door. By this time, lingerers shouldn't stay longer than it takes to snuff out their cigarettes.

Q. *I recently gave a buffet luncheon for sixteen women. Two women were over an hour late, yet they didn't even make an effort to call me. I was late serving lunch and several guests could not stay for dessert or coffee. What can I do if this happens again?*

A. Do not delay serving your guests because of two thoughtless women. Serve on schedule just as you had planned. It's often expected that guests will be fifteen minutes late finding your house the first time but anything more, even for a newcomer, is uncalled for in my opinion.

Q. *My husband and I gave a dinner party last week that totally unnerved me. My table seats a maximum of eight.*

60

*We invited three couples which made a total of eight counting us. One couple showed up at our door with their house guest and said, "I know you won't mind, one more doesn't make any difference and it's always such fun to have an extra man." It did make a difference in every way. We can seat only eight and I only have service for eight in my good china, silver, and crystal. I had made eight individual desserts. I gave the uninvited guest my place at the table while I squeezed in on his left and ate from a salad plate. My evening was ruined, yet they acted perfectly happy with the situation. What can a hostess do?*

**A.** No more or less than you did. I applaud you for your handling of this delicate situation. Now a word to that thoughtless couple who brought along the extra guest—you were rude and insensitive to do this to your hostess. No guest should bring another guest to a dinner party without clearing this with the host or hostess. Furthermore, an invited guest should not put the host or hostess on the spot by asking to bring someone. The inviting should be left up to the hostess. Once she knows you have a houseguest and is silent, you should realize that another guest cannot be accommodated. For a cocktail party or buffet supper, a host or hostess can be more flexible and add more guests if desired.

# Guest Duties

**Q.** *I keep reading and hearing about the duties of the host and hostess. How about the guests who sit like bumps on a* *log all evening and make little or no effort at conversation? Don't guests have duties too?*

A. Yes. A guest's contribution is, in most instances, as important as the efforts of the hostess. The host and hostess have supplied the place, the food, the drink, all niceties to make a party. It's the responsibility of the guest to furnish interesting conversation and to look as attractive as possible. Each guest should make an effort to mingle and speak to other guests. If making conversation is a problem, read and practice Barbara Walter's book, *How To Talk With Practically Anybody About Practically Anything.*

Q. *Can you give some hints on party manners for a guest?*

A. Greet your host and hostess first but don't monopolize them. Introduce yourself to others if your host is busy. Try to mingle with all the guests. Avoid separating into groups of the same sex. Don't take up your host and hostess's time with long goodbyes.

# Guest Bathrooms

Q. *I've noticed after our parties that finger towels are rarely touched in our bathrooms. Why?*

A. I can't give you a reason for this strange phenomenon. I see the same thing at my house. To all guests every-where—if you use the bathroom, wash your hands and do use the towels provided.

**Q.** *When guests use our bathroom they always leave the top of the toilet seat up. How can I let them know that I prefer it down?*

**A.** Stencil on the lid *Put Me Down.*

**Q.** *Where do I put a linen or terrycloth finger towel after using it in a private home? I want to do the correct thing.*

**A.** There is no correct place to put the dirty towel. If there is a counter space near the sink, place it there, or hang it unfolded on a corner of the rack. One hostess I know provides a small wicker basket for soiled towels.

# Gifts

**Q.** *Sometimes when we entertain, a guest will bring a gift. I never know whether to open the gift in front of the others, or put it aside. What is proper?*

**A.** Quietly thank the donor, put the gift aside to be opened later. Never open the gift nor show it in front of the other guests. They will be embarrassed that they didn't bring something. Within a few days thank the donor again, by note or telephone.

**Q.** *We recently moved into a new house and gave an open-house party. Several friends brought gifts—two gifts had no card or anything indicating the donor. Now I don't know whom to thank. Please comment.*

**A.** Any gift taken to a party should always include a card or a note with the donor's name. At most parties, the hosts are so busy greeting guests that they cannot be expected to remember who brought which gift.

# Gifts of Food

**Q.** *At our last dinner party a guest brought a dish of shrimp paté and some crackers. I did not serve her paté because I had already prepared appetizers. The next day she called to thank me and asked why I hadn't served her delicious shrimp. I was embarrassed and said, "I am saving it for tonight when the neighbors come for drinks." Please comment about guests who bring food without making arrangements with the hostess.*

**A.** Guests should never bring food unless it has been prearranged. The host or hostess has planned the menu, and anything extra, no matter how delicious, might confuse the plans.

# Flowers

**Q.** *What can I do with a bunch of flowers thrust into my hands by a well-meaning guest? I simply didn't have time to* *arrange them, and my vases were all in use. I stuck them in a milk bottle and put them aside. Isn't there another gift less troublesome to take a hostess?*

A. Yes, there is. Anything small and inexpensive such as guest soaps, notepaper, or recipe cards. Flowers can be troublesome for the hostess who does all of her work and is expecting more guests to ring the doorbell any minute. I recommend only taking cut flowers already arranged in a container.

Q. *I was recently told never to arrive at a party with flowers. I asked why not and was told, "It simply is not done these days." Can you supply a clearer answer?*

A. Few households have servants today. Therefore, it means that the hostess has to find a vase and arrange the flowers in the midst of her other greetings and preparations. Have the flowers sent ahead of time or take them arranged in a container.

# New Acquaintances

Q. *My husband and I are very fond of a couple we've known about a year, and they seem genuinely fond of us. We have entertained them at our house with seated dinners, buffets, and patio cookouts. They have never refused an invitation we extended but they have never extended any type of invitation to us. In fact, we've never been in their* house and they live in our neighborhood. I am a bit hurt and perplexed by their actions. What do you think?

A. I think they are "takers" not willing to give hospitality. If we accept the hospitality of our friends we should be willing to return it. Are they really friends or moochers?

Q. My husband and I met a very attractive couple at a friend's house. We later invited them to dinner at our house, but didn't invite our friends since we see them so often. Now they are angry and say we were wrong to not include them. Are we wrong?

A. Yes. Never invite the "Newly Mets" unless you invite the host and hostess that brought you together. It's not necessary to include them after the first time.

Q. We have lived in this area for almost a year and now we want to reach out and develop some friendships. What do you recommend?

A. A party. It's the easiest way to develop friendships. Of course there are many ways of reaching out to people, and a party may seem to be a frivolous way to do so. However, there are people who will respond to an invitation to a party but will reject other overtures of friendship. Good luck.

Q. When we entertain at our house, we try to bring new friends into our group, but none of our old friends will try to develop a friendship with these newcomers. Consequently when they entertain we see the same people over and over. Can you offer a solution?

A. Entertaining the same people whom you know and like all the time gets to be like the Wednesday night bridge club. You know them and they know you, and there is nothing stimulating about it. Keep bringing in new faces. Perhaps the old faces will get the picture sooner or later.

Q. *My husband pesters me to invite to dinner people we barely know. He claims we need new friends and more exposure to other people. I feel comfortable with our old friends and I have no need to make new friends. What do you think?*

A. I think you live in a very small world, which is obviously what your husband is trying to tell you. Entertaining is done to widen one's circle of friends and acquaintances. You gain a lot of knowledge by exposure to new people. Try it!

# Friends from Other Countries

Q. *I have only lived in this country for a few months. My English is pretty good, but I am very confused by certain terms, i.e., "We are having the Joneses for dinner." This sounds so strange. Is it correct?*

A. No. Only cannibals "have people for dinner." One should say, "The Joneses are coming to dinner."

Q. *As a newcomer to this country I am baffled. Do you Americans really mean it when you say, "Come to see me?"*

**A.** No. "Come to see me" is a friendly expression which can be interpreted to mean the person would enjoy seeing you again. It does not constitute an invitation. You might respond by saying, "That would be very nice. Please let me know when it would be convenient for you."

**Q.** *I am Italian and I have been in this wonderful country for three years. I love America and its people, but I wish our friends wouldn't serve us Italian foods when they invite us to dinner. Why is this done?*

**A.** Probably it's an effort to try to please you and to show you that they love Italians and Italian foods. However, the best rule of thumb is the following: don't serve Italian foods to Italians, don't serve German foods to Germans etc. Share an American meal with your friends from other countries.

# Living Abroad

**Q.** *My husband and I will be living in another country for three years. Should we entertain in our American style or try to imitate the country's custom?*

**A.** Entertain in the American manner. You will have more confidence and your guests of the host country will be interested in learning American customs.

**Q.** *We are going to live in a South American country for three years. A woman casually mentioned that in all Latin* *countries there is a place of honor in the living room for the guest of honor. I know there is a place of honor at the table but I've never heard of this before. True or false?*

**A.** True. There is a place of honor for the guest of honor in the living room—on the right hand side of the sofa, as you sit. This custom is practiced in many European and South American countries and in protocol conscious Washington.

**Q.** *We will be stationed in a foreign country for several years. Should I salute the foreign flag? What should I do when our host country's national anthem is played?*

**A.** No, do not salute the foreign flag. Stand at attention with your hands at your side for both.

# Home Entertaining

Dorothea Johnson

# Host and Hostess

**Q.** *Please list some basic duties for a host and hostess.*

**A.** When the party begins, the host or hostess, preferably both, opens the door and greets each guest. If the hosts are in conversation with other guests when the doorbell rings, they must excuse themselves to greet the new arrivals. Duties include at least a brief conversation with each guest. Once guests have made the first move to go, the hosts help them find their coats, lead the way to the door and open it for them.

**Q.** *Would you please comment about the host or hostess who slams the door the minute a guest departs. I always feel they are glad to see us leave.*

**A.** If the hosts live in a house, they should stand at the doorway until the guests have reached the sidewalk or their cars. In an apartment building, the hosts should watch from the apartment door until the guests are a distance down the hall or on the elevator.

Dorothea Johnson

# Tit for Tat

**Q.** *My husband's boss and his wife invited us to a dinner party in their beautiful home. Everything was elegant and perfect . . . a soup course, roast beef . . . the works. I want to invite them to our house, which is modest by their standards, but tastefully decorated. Must I serve the same type of dinner they served us?*

**A.** No. Entertaining should be what's fun for you and feasible for your lifestyle. Serve what you do well—be it beef stew or tuna casserole.

**Q.** *Should a dinner obligation always be repaid with a dinner?*

**A.** No. Today you can repay an elaborate dinner with a hotdog—hamburger cookout or a cocktail buffet. Any type of entertaining that is feasible for your lifestyle and financial capabilities is appropriate. No apologies are necessary.

# Nervous Hostess

**Q.** *When we invite guests to dinner I get very nervous. The food, the house, everything is in order except me. How* *about some tips for a "nervous Nellie" that would help me feel more at ease and poised.*

**A.** Walk slowly and avoid excessive movement such as using your hands too much while talking. Practice keeping them still. Don't talk or laugh too loud or too much. Don't bite your nails, chain smoke, or play with your hair.

# Have Nots

**Q.** *We went to a dinner party Saturday night that was very disturbing. Our hosts have recently moved into a new house, therefore many items of furniture and accessories need to be added which I know will take time. They spent the evening showing pictures of every item they plan to purchase, and apologizing for not already having these things. Needless to say it was a boring evening because none of the guests were allowed to contribute to the conversation. What do you think?*

**A.** Your host and hostess not only brought attention to these needed, but lacking, items, but bored their guests in the telling. I think it's just as tacky to complain about what one doesn't have as it is to brag about what one does have.

Dorothea Johnson

# Caterers

**Q.** *As a widow who has been entertained by numerous friends, I want to reciprocate and entertain them in my home. But each time I have made the effort I get so nervous that it takes me a week to recover. I can't eat or sleep the night before so I am usually weak and exhausted. Therefore, I usually take the coward's way out by taking everyone to a restaurant. What do you recommend?*

**A.** A caterer. One can eliminate all of your worries. A caterer will sit down with you and plan any type of party. They will handle everything for you—invitations, centerpiece, tablesetting, preparation of food in your kitchen or theirs, serving, and cleaning up. All you have to do is look pretty and be the smiling, calm, and confident hostess.

# Kitchen Syndrome

**Q.** *Our guests always gather in my kitchen. I don't want them there but I don't know how to tactfully let them know it's off limits.*

**A.** To avoid "kitchen syndrome," set out the drinks on a table in the living room. Appetizers can be served there and the serving of the meal confined to the dining room. Keep the kitchen doors closed.

Dorothea Johnson

# Helping the Hostess

**Q.** *I love to entertain and frankly do not like guests in my tiny kitchen. One women guest always jumps up and proceeds to create havoc at the table and in the kitchen. I feel helpless, but what can I do?*

**A.** Firmly, but gently, tell her you do not want any help. You might add in a friendly way that you don't expect to work when you go to her house.

# Early Birds

**Q.** *What can I do if people arrive too early for a dinner party I have planned?*

**A.** Just pretend you are delighted to see them, but naturally carry on with what you are doing to finish preparing for the party. It is best to have everything ready and under control at least thirty minutes before your guests are due to arrive. The thoughtful guest will be ten minutes late instead of ten minutes early.

# Social Debts

**Q.** *I have been invited to numerous parties this past year. For one reason or another I have not repaid any of my social obligations. Now I feel I owe everyone. Can I give one huge party at my country club and consider everyone paid back?*

**A.** I hope you will not try to wipe out all your social obligations at one fell swoop. Guests catch on quickly to your motives. Consider several smaller parties which will permit you to spend time with your guests. Duplicate menus and decorations to make the multiple parties less of a burden to you.

**Q.** *Can you offer some hints on keeping my parties organized so that I will not repeat menus and guests?*

**A.** Keep a party record book. Record your menu, the date and the guest list. Note drink preference of guests, dishes that drew raves, who sat next to whom, what you wore, and any other details that would be helpful for future party planning. See the Party Record chapter at the end of this book. It not only shows how such a record can be kept, but even provides sample forms for your use.

Dorothea Johnson

# Serving Refreshments

**Q.** *When someone visits me in my home should I ask if they want refreshments or should I just go ahead and serve them?*

**A.** Prepare refreshments in advance and serve them. It's impolite to put the burden on the guest by asking if they want something.

# Greeting Guests

**Q.** *Does a host or hostess stand when greeting a guest?*

**A.** Yes, always, and when they depart too.

# Confident Entertaining

**Q.** *As a hostess, how can I really tell if my latest party was a success? Days later I keep asking myself, "Was it a good party, did my guests enjoy it?"*

79

A. Did you enjoy your party? Did you have a good time? If your answer is yes, the guests did too!

# Group Arrival

Q. *When we entertain at our house I get confused when a group of guests arrive at the same time. How do I greet them?*

A. If several guests arrive simultaneously, greet those nearest you first. If most of the women are about the same age, greet them in a clockwise direction. Greet each guest with the same amount of warmth and enthusiasm.

# Preparty Planning

Q. *We recently went to a dinner party and met some very nice and interesting people. The person I wanted to know better, the hostess, spent most of the evening in the kitchen. This incident made me realize I am guilty of the same thing. Please tell me how to handle this situation so I can spend more time with my guests.*

**A.** Preparty planning. Plan a meal that can be prepared in advance, one that needs only heating in the oven, i.e., chicken and rice casserole. The salad can be prepared ahead and tossed at the last minute. Serve a dessert such as a cold souffle that can be made a day ahead and refrigerated or made several days ahead and frozen.

# Ingredients for a Good Party

**Q.** *What are the ingredients of a good party?*

**A.** People—ambiance—planning. Plan a menu with as little preparation as possible to be done after guests arrive. There is nothing less attractive than talking to a host or hostess whose thoughts are elsewhere. Plan—then your mind will be free to enjoy your guests.

# Party Division

**Q.** *It happened again last night! We were ten married couples invited to dinner at a neighbor's anniversary party. Men were on one side of the room and women on the other. Why does this always happen, and is there a solution?*

**A.** This probably happens because traditionally, we've been divided in roles and jobs along sex lines. That situation at a party is a reflection of this division. I think we will see less of this as women develop more interests outside the home. This is not so common in larger cities. Unfortunately, many men still think women are capable of only making "small talk." I know one solution that works. Simply walk into the group of men and say, "You seem to be having such an interesting conversation that I want to join you." Keep up with current events so that you can make interesting and intelligent conversation. Hosts and hostesses can help by bringing men into groups of women and vice versa.

# Coffees

**Q.** *We moved into a new neighborhood three months ago and much to my surprise only two neighbors have called on me. I want to give a coffee or tea to get acquainted with our neighbors. Is this proper even though they haven't called on me?*

**A.** Yes. By all means go ahead and give your coffee or tea. We are much more flexible about these things today and don't necessarily stand on tradition. Use your calling card, post card, plain or engraved notepaper. Call it a "Neighborhood Get-Acquainted Coffee." Add your name, address and telephone number. Since you don't know your neighbor's names, just put each invitation in a plain envelope, take a walk, and drop one in each mailbox. They may not even know the custom that they should call first, or they may not be aware that you are a new neighbor.

# Candles

**Q.** *I am planning a large neighborhood coffee this winter. May I use candles if the day is cold and dreary?*

**A.** No. Candles are not used at a coffee or a luncheon. Use them for teas, but draw your curtains even though it is still daytime outside. Naturally, they add atmosphere to any evening entertainment.

# Dinners

## Labeling Your Party

**Q.** *I am confused by the terms* Dinner *and* Supper. *Don't they mean the same thing?*

**A.** Yes, but keep in mind that the label you pin on your party tells the guests what to expect. *Dinner* means a sit down meal at a set hour. *Supper* indicates a lighter and more informal meal. Either can be served by the host or hostess. However, if you label it *Buffet supper,* the guests serve themselves.

## *Serving*

**Q.** *I always thought waiters served from the left and took away from the right. Now I see them serving and removing from the left. Which is correct?*

**A.** Both methods are acceptable now. Pouring wiⅰe and removing glasses are always done from the right.

## *Appetizer Etiquette*

**Q.** *I was at a dinner party recently and noted that a guest took several hors d'oeuvres when they were passed. By the time the hostess got to me they were all gone. Is there appetizer etiquette for a greedy guest?*

**A.** Appetizer etiquette follows: Don't take more than one hors d'oeuvre from a tray before the tray has gone around.

## *Waiters*

**Q.** *I am a self-employed waiter who works in private homes. Usually I start work about five P.M., and finish up about one A.M. I help the hostess with any last minute work that needs my attention and set up the bar. Guests start arriving about 7:30 P.M. Rarely am I offered any food before or after a party. Should my employer offer me food or should I help myself to whatever is available?*

**A.** The thoughtful employer will indeed tell a waiter to feel free to prepare himself something to eat before or after a party. If this doesn't happen you are free to ask if you can prepare yourself something.

## *Dinner is Served*

**Q.** *When I announce, "Dinner is served," my guests are usually ready for food but tend to hang back. What can I do tactfully to get my guests into the dining room quickly?*

**A.** Ringing a small dinner bell is a charming attention-getter. For a seated dinner, your husband should be ready to escort into the dining room the woman who will sit on his right. For a buffet, the hostess should indicate the woman she wishes to start the buffet, usually the eldest and most distinguished woman present.

## *When Dinner Guests Start Eating*

**Q.** *At a seated dinner party, and at a buffet supper, when do the guests start eating?*

**A.** At a very small dinner they should wait until everyone is served, unless the hosts urge them to begin right away because the food may get cold. At a seated dinner of ten or more they start as soon as those next to them have been served. At a buffet supper where tables seat four or six people, wait until one or two others have sat down. At a buffet supper eaten on laps, each person begins as soon as he finds a place to sit.

Dorothea Johnson

## *Serving Coffee*

**Q.** *I like to serve coffee after dinner in our living room. Recently a guest asked me for coffee during dinner. I wasn't prepared for his request and said, "Coffee will be served later." My husband said I was wrong, that I should have honored my guest's request. Shouldn't a guest wait for the hostess to offer coffee? Incidentally, I had wine and water on the table so it wasn't a question of not having anything to drink.*

**A.** A guest should always wait and see what the hostess is offering. Your husband is wrong, although I'm sure his intent was to be hospitable. Just remember that when you entertain, you are the director—you are in charge. If it's your method to serve coffee after dinner in the living room, do so.

# *Luncheon*

**Q.** *Recently I attended a luncheon and the hostess dominated the conversation talking about how hard she had worked getting everything together. "I was up until 2 A.M. and I am exhausted." On and on she went until I felt terrible and the other guests acted very uncomfortable. Should we have been told all the gory details of her preparty toils?*

**A.** Never. The thoughtful, considerate hostess will spare her guests any unpleasantries she encountered while getting her party together and that includes the work involved. She should act as if it were a breeze even though we all know the effort put forth.

# Pouring at Teas

**Q.** *I have heard that Europeans do not pour at their teas and that we should never ask them to pour at ours. Please comment.*

**A.** An employee pours and serves the tea in most of the European countries. When you ask someone from another country "to pour," explain that this is an American custom which is considered an honor.

**Q.** *I've been asked to pour at a large formal tea. I'm uncertain about the procedure of pouring and what to say to the recipient of the cup of tea. Please comment.*

**A.** Pour the cup three-fourths full to prevent spilling, then you ask, "Sugar? Milk or lemon?" These go in after you pour the tea. Note that milk is offered instead of cream. Milk is better because the fat content of cream smothers the tea flavor.

Dorothea Johnson

# Guest of Honor

**Q.** *I gave a tea for the wife of my husband's boss. They are being transferred and I felt this would be a good opportunity for her to say goodbye to many friends. I had planned to stand with her in the foyer and greet guests as they came in. She was over an hour late and I didn't know if I should start serving tea or wait. I waited but it was difficult keeping the women from the tea table. What would you have done?*

**A.** I would have waited about fifteen minutes and then started serving tea. When the honored guest arrived I would have quietly announced her arrival and told everyone that she and I would be in the foyer to greet friends.

# Teabags

**Q.** *How do I gracefully handle a teabag when it's served in a cup of tea?*

**A.** Remove it from the teacup and place on the saucer or butter plate. Do not attempt to drain teabag. Never wind or twirl string around the spoon to drain.

Dorothea Johnson

# Nametags

**Q.** *Do women wear nametags at a tea?*

**A.** Quite often at large teas held in clubs nametags are worn. This is usually the choice of the chairman or hostess of the group. They are not worn at small teas in private homes.

# Open House

**Q.** *We have moved into a lovely new home. I want to give an open house and invite some friends from my husband's law firm office and some of our new neighbors. My husband does not want to mix the two groups. What do you recommend?*

**A.** Do not bunch people in categories—all your lawyer friends or all your new neighbors. It's best not to invite an entire clique or group of close friends at one time. I think your open house will prove more interesting to you, your husband, and your friends—lawyers and neighbors—to introduce them all to each other.

**Q.** *We moved into a new home and I want to give a house-warming party but I don't want guests to feel they*

89

*have to bring gifts. Can I write* no gifts *on the invitation?*

**A.** Do not put *no gifts* on your invitation. Instead of labeling your party as a house warming, which almost cries for a gift, call it an open house. In my opinion, "open house" is the better term to use when you want to welcome a lot of friends into a new home for the first time.

# Cocktail Party

**Q.** *A couple in our neighborhood gave a cocktail party. During the party I heard the hostess whisper to several guests, "Stay for supper when the rest leave." What do you think of this?*

**A.** I think it should be a forthright cocktail party with snacks or a cocktail buffet—for everybody.

# Cocktail Buffet

**Q.** *We are giving a cocktail buffet for fifty people. I want to serve a large ham, but rather than slice it thinly in the traditional manner, I would like to present it with style and flair. What do you suggest?*

**A.** Consider "porcupine ham." Cut a huge slab from the bottom of a baked ham, almost half of it, right up to the bone. Decorate a platter with lots of leafy greens and place the remainder of the ham on the platter with the round side up. Cut the slab of ham into cubes and spear each cube with a toothpick and then stick it into the whole ham. Repeat until the ham is covered with cubes. Garnish the platter with several bunches of grapes. For a smaller party, use a pineapple as a base for the cubed ham. A whole melon is a perfect cushion with melon and ham on a toothpick. Use your imagination and create unusual combinations. Most fruits go well with ham.

# Buffets

**Q.** *I am planning a cocktail buffet for about fifty people. Will I need to provide a place to sit for everyone?*

**A.** No. A rule of thumb for chairs at large parties—have half as many chairs as you have guests. This will keep some people circulating and thus prevent a stagnating situation where everyone is seated. It will also allow enough space to move around comfortably.

Dorothea Johnson

# Buffet Supper

**Q.** *I felt my last buffet supper was a flop. All the women went through the line, then all the men. The women sat on one side of the room and the men on the other side. I see this at buffets all the time. Don't people know they should mingle or was I at fault for not insisting?*

**A.** You were at fault. As a hostess you are the director. Let your guests know what you expect of them. Pass out escort cards to all the men. They are one by two inch cards in an envelope and are stocked by most department stores and stationers. Put a man's name on the envelope and a woman's on the card inside. This way they go through the buffet line together and sit together. After all, if this were a seated dinner the hostess would establish the seating arrangements. So why not do so at a buffet supper. I've seen it work successfully at buffet brunches, luncheons, and suppers where both sexes were present.

**Q.** *At a recent buffet supper, the butter was ice cold and very hard to cut. Shouldn't butter be served at room temperature?*

**A.** Softened butter is tastier, and much easier to serve and spread, but avoid letting it stand at room temperature any longer than necessary. Butter's delicate flavor and its vitamin A content will be affected adversely if it is left standing too long in temperatures above fifty degrees Fahrenheit where light and air can get to it. To serve butter, mound it in a glass or porcelain dish, cover tightly with saran wrap and keep refrigerated until about one hour before using.

**Q.** *At buffet suppers I sometimes see guests pile food on their plate. Often they can't eat all that's on the plate and it's wasted. Please comment on this unsightly and wasteful habit.*

**A.** It's best to skimp on one's plate than take more food than can be eaten. Several trips to the buffet are proper and the host and hostess will consider it a compliment. It's not necessary to sample all of the dishes at an elaborate buffet. Save room for dessert.

# Wine Tasting and Buffet Supper

**Q.** *I want to give a wine tasting party for ten couples. Several couples must drive for over an hour to reach our house and I don't feel that wine and cheese are enough. Can you suggest an alternative?*

**A.** You are correct in feeling that cheese and wine are not sufficient for such a long trip. Try my method. My husband and I give this type of party often and call it "Wine tasting and buffet supper." Offer an assortment of cheeses and plain crackers with the wines. Then a hearty meal-in-one-dish casserole, green salad, dessert, and coffee. Your party can be as simple or as elaborate as you choose.

# Table Talk

# Table Manners

**Q.** *Why is it considered bad manners to take anything to drink while there is food in the mouth? Often, I feel it helps to wash the food down.*

**A.** This may leave particles of food in the beverage or a smear on the glass. Both are unattractive. Food should never be "washed down." The mouth should be empty before taking anything to drink.

# Arms on Table

**Q.** *I am hoping you can settle a long-standing argument between a friend and myself. I would like to know if it is correct to place both forearms on the edge of a table or counter when eating.*

**A.** No, I don't consider it correct to place the forearms on a table or counter nor is it very attractive. If you feel a need to rest on the table, place the wrist lightly on the table. It's more comfortable and attractive to sit with the base of your

97

spine against the back of your chair and your feet flat on the floor. Elbows on the table are permissible between courses but not while one is eating.

# Saying Grace

Q. *At our house, it is a custom for my husband to say grace before each meal. He would like to occasionally ask an honored guest to say grace but does not know how to approach him or her. What is proper?*

A. Ask the guest in advance to say the blessing, never at the last minute. Then at the table your husband could say, "Mr. Smith, or Ms. Jones, would you please honor us by saying the blessing tonight?"

# Second Helpings

Q. *How can I tactfully offer my guest second helpings or more food without using the words* second helping *or* more food?

A. Say, "Would you like roast beef?"

Dorothea Johnson

# Eating Utensils

Q. *We recently moved to the Washington, D.C., area. Because of my husband's job we were invited to dinner at one of the embassies. I was confused by all the eating utensils and had never seen a fork and spoon placed above the dinner plate. Please comment on this so others will be spared my embarrassment.*

A. The table is set with flatware arranged in the order of use—from the outside in. For whatever course comes first, you'll need the utensil on the extreme right or left; for the next course the next utensil in and so on. If it is a formal dinner the server will remove any forks, spoons, or knives that are unnecessary, after each course. Then the correct utensil will be next in line. The fork and spoon above the plate is for dessert.

# Toothpicks

Q. *Is it correct for me to place toothpicks in a holder on the table for my dinner guests? Also when and where is it proper for a person to use a toothpick?*

A. No. Do not place toothpicks on the table. In this country one uses a toothpick only in private. Many Europeans consider it proper to use a toothpick, screening the mouth with a table napkin. The Japanese use the hand as a screen.

If a tiny bone or shell gets lodged and you can't remove it with your tongue (without facial distortions), excuse yourself quietly from the table and go to the bathroom and remove the offending bit. No explanations are necessary when you return.

I think the most sensible place for toothpicks is in the bathroom. Stim-U-Dents are available in drug stores and the wise men and women carry their own.

# Smoking

## At Table

**Q.** *What is the basic rule for smoking at table?*

**A.** If there are no ashtrays on the table, this means no smoking. If ashtrays are provided light up a cigarette only when the dessert course has been finished.

**Q.** *I recently gave a seated luncheon in my home for several women. Since I do not like smoking at the table I do not put out ashtrays. Otherwise I don't mind if guests smoke. While I was serving dessert one guest got up from the table, returned with an ashtray and proceeded to smoke. Is there some way I can tactfully let guests know I don't want them to smoke during the meal?*

**A.** You were tactfully telling your guests not to smoke when you did not put ashtrays on the table. Now a word to the smoker. It is the height of rudeness for a guest to bring an ashtray to the table and smoke. Wait until the meal is over and you've left the table.

**Q.** *At our last dinner party a guest took his awful-smelling pipe to the dining room and laid it on the table by his placemat. I noticed this bothered the woman on his left so when I served the first course I removed the pipe and said, "This just doesn't go with my table decor." My husband thinks I was wrong. Was I?*

**A.** No. I think you were very clever in your handling of this smelly matter. A guest should never take a pipe or lighted cigarette to the table.

**Q.** *At my last seated dinner party I was ready to serve dessert when the guest on my left announced to me that he had to have a smoke. He then left the dining room and returned with an ashtray and proceeded to smoke. I was speechless. Now I am furious for permitting this annoyance to the other guests and myself. What could I have tactfully said?*

**A.** He made the announcement to you, the hostess. At that moment you should have said, "I am just starting to serve dessert, please wait until everyone has eaten theirs."

## At Parties

**Q.** *I have guests who put their cigarettes out in my coffee cups. What can I do?*

**A.** Firmly, but gently, place an ashtray within reach and say, "Please use this."

**Q.** *About a week ago we went to a large cocktail party. On the front door was a* No Smoking Please *sign. Inside were similar signs in both rooms where the party took place. Several of the guests who smoke and I were annoyed that we had to stand around and drink for two hours and were not able to smoke. Don't you think this was rude and unfair of the host and hostess?*

**A.** No, I do not. It's their home and they establish the rules which you as a guest should accept.

## Cigarette Lighting

**Q.** *When it comes to lighting cigarettes my husband has the fastest lighter in the country for every woman but me. He claims other women come first in this matter. I feel I should. Who is right?*

**A.** You are. The wife or date has precedence when it comes to cigarette lighting. If a man is the host, his guest of honor or an older woman gets her cigarette lit first. Today many women are prepared to light their own cigarettes without comment.

# Table Decor

## Table Linens

**Q.** *When may I use my wash-and-wear Quaker Lace tablecloth?*

**A.** For coffees or teas when you want to present a pretty table. Seated dinner parties and buffet suppers. I prefer not to see this type of cloth on a luncheon table.

**Q.** *My nice table linens were destroyed in a fire. Now my house is back in order and I want to do some entertaining but find the table linens too expensive to replace. Can you suggest something attractive and inexpensive?*

**A.** Consider sheets. They look better than wash and wear linens, there is more variety in colors, and they're inexpensive. Try covering a table to the floor. Buy an extra sheet for napkins. From one twin size, flat sheet you can make a dozen twenty inch by twenty inch napkins. I call them "lapkins" and they are great for seated dinners or buffet suppers. Look in the home decorating magazines for colorful and elegant tableclothes and napkins made from sheets or inexpensive fabrics.

## Napkins

**Q.** *Where should the napkins be placed when I set my table to entertain guests?*

A. There are no rules for informal tablesettings. You can stuff napkins in the wine glasses, tie in a knot and place above the place setting, place in the center of the mat or the right or left. Anyplace is suitable just as long as it looks pretty and is in harmony with the place setting. For a formal table setting, the napkin is folded and placed on the service plate.

Q. *What can I do about women friends who blot their lips on my best linen napkins when they dine at my house? Can I tactfully mention it?*

A. No. Say nothing. However, try my method. I insert a small four by four inch red cotton napkin inside of the white napkin at each place setting where a woman guest will be seated. They quickly get the message. Creates conversation too. Make these "lip blotters" from a loosely woven cotton, linen or polyester fabric. Use a zigzag stitch about one-half inch from the edge, then start fringing.

Q. *Would you please give some clear and simple advice about napkins? Unfolding a small and large napkin? Where do I put the napkin if I must leave the table during a meal and where do I place my napkin when I've finished eating?*

A. Unfold a breakfast or luncheon (small) napkin to its full size. Leave a large dinner napkin folded in half and place it over your lap without a flourish. At the end of the meal, pick up the napkin by the center, gather it together loosely, and place it at the left of the plate. Should you have to leave the table briefly, follow the same procedure. Paper napkins get the same treatment as linen ones. At a family meal, a cloth napkin may be refolded to use again.

Q. *When is it proper to tuck a dinner napkin in one's collar?*

A. Never.

## Centerpiece

Q. *How high should a centerpiece be on my luncheon or dinner table?*

A. For a buffet brunch, luncheon, or supper, height or size doesn't matter. For a seated brunch, luncheon, or dinner, make your centerpiece low so that guests will have no trouble seeing each other. There is nothing more distressing than to sit through a luncheon or dinner staring at a view-blocking floral arrangement. Instead of a large centerpiece of fresh flowers, small flower units; ornaments of glass, silver, china; or fruits or vegetables may be used. A stack of unusual or handsomely bound books, twined with ivy, arranged in the center of a table is a unique conversational centerpiece.

Q. *We have a pumpkin in our garden which is the pride of our children. We want to use it as a centerpiece for our Thanksgiving dinner and keep it as long as possible. Can it be treated to last several weeks?*

A. Yes. Cut about a third of the pumpkin from the top in a sawtooth or smooth design. Scrape the pumpkin out very clean, then pour melted paraffin wax in and roll it around to coat the inside wall. Wait several minutes, then spray the pumpkin with a light coat of clear shellac and let dry. A container of fresh fall flowers set in the shell will last for days and may be renewed as often as necessary. An arrangement of dried flowers will last as long as the pumpkin holds up, several weeks to two months. The longevity is determined by the temperature in your house.

# Candles

**Q.** *I'm not sure about the lighting of candles on my dinner table. Do I light them before the guests sit down or after they are seated? When are they extinguished?*

**A.** Candles are lighted just before the guests enter the dining room. They are extinguished after all the guests have left the table.

# Service Plates

**Q.** *I inherited twelve silver service plates from my grandmother who used them regularly. It is my understanding that the service plate is removed when the main course is served, but I would like to leave them on the table throughout the meal. May I?*

**A.** Yes. Just place the dinner plate on the service plate. Traditional rules for using china, crystal and silver need no longer apply. In today's tablesettings, personal expression is the only rule.

# Soup Tureens

**Q.** *I have three lovely old tureens in my storage closet. I never serve soup so they are not used. Can you suggest some way I can use them?*

**Q.** Your tureens can be used in many ways. Serve your main course from one—stroganoff, beef burgandy stew or chicken ala king. Use them for serving tossed, potato, or bean salads or for vegetables. They are also attractive as decorative accessories in a dining room or kitchen. Tureens also make marvelous containers for flowers as a centerpiece, or try a potted plant in one.

# Placecards

**Q.** *My husband and I attended a dinner party where there was a lot of confusion at the dinner table because there were no placecards and the hostess said, "Just sit anyplace." Shouldn't a hostess indicate who sits where?*

**A.** Yes, the hostess should always tell you which chair is yours. Placecards eliminate confusion for the hosts and guests.

**Q.** *When there are no placecards on a dinner table and the hostess says, "Sit anyplace," who sits where?*

**A.** It is totally unfair for a hostess to say, "Sit anyplace." In seating guests, it is the responsibility of the host or hostess to tell each one where to sit. It is customary for the host and hostess to be on opposite ends of the table. Usually the woman guest of honor sits at the immediate right of the host. The man guest of honor sits to the immediate right of the hostess. Placecards eliminate confusion on the part of hosts and guests.

# Seating

**Q.** *We are planning a seated buffet supper for Christmas Eve. There will be sixteen of us so I will rent two round tables and seat eight at each table. I am uncertain about the seating because I've not used this two table arrangement before. What do you recommend?*

**A.** Seat your husband at one table and yourself at the other one. The guest of honor should sit on your right and his wife or date on your husband's right, second man on your left and second woman on your husband's left. Be sure place cards are used to eliminate confusion for you and your guests.

**Q.** *We are going to entertain my husband's boss, his wife, and another couple. How should I seat the six of us at the table?*

**A.** Seat your husband's boss at your right and the other male guest on your left. Seat the boss's wife on your husband's right and the other female guest on his left.

# Guest of Honor

**Q.** *When there is a guest of honor at a dinner is he or she the first or last to leave?*

**A.** The guest of honor is the first to leave.

# *Dieting*

**Q.** *Due to a stomach disorder I can't eat anything but bland foods. I don't want to give up dinner parties completely. Can you offer a solution?*

**A.** Eat your bland diet before going out. When dinner is served, move the food around on the plate and make brilliant conversation. If this solution isn't feasible for you, tell the hostess your problem and say that you would like to drop in after the meal is over.

**Q.** *I am on a diet for weight control, but I don't want to eliminate going to or giving dinner parties. What can I do?*

**A.** Cut down on calorie intake before and after a party. Take smaller portions but try some of everything.

**Q.** *Please comment about guests on diets who won't eat after I've spent hours preparing a gourmet dinner.*

**A.** If a guest is on a diet, no one minds a "No, thanks," to appetizers, bread, and potatoes. But don't sit with an empty plate however fattening the menu. It's always polite to take a little helping of food you don't like or don't wish to eat and push it around the plate. The implied, "Look at me and my will power," may depress your dinner partners who want to enjoy the dinner and the calories. If the problem is medical, please tell your hostess ahead of time so she won't be offended.

# Small Appetites

**Q.** *I am not a large eater, but often at seated dinners the hostess will pile my plate with food. It's embarrassing when I can't even eat a fourth of it, and I do want to save room for dessert. Friends of mine complain about this too. Please comment.*

**A.** Moderation is part of good manners. It's always best to offer second helpings rather than fill a plate. The thoughtful host or hostess will put a moderate amount on the plate when she serves—ditto the guest, if it's a buffet. Nothing looks worse than a heaping plate. Remember it's a compliment to the host and hostess when you ask for or go for a second helping.

**Q.** *I'm not a large eater, yet I find it difficult to refuse seconds because I don't want to hurt my hostess' feelings. What can I say to let her know I've enjoyed every morsel but don't care for seconds?*

**A.** Say, "No, thank you. It was a delicious dinner." Never say, "I'm full," or "I'm stuffed."

# Allergies

**Q.** *What can a host or hostess do when guests accept an invitation to dinner, then when it's served, announce they* *have such and such allergies? I have had this happen to me twice in the past month.*

**A.** It's best to serve meat and fowl dishes. Save seafood for those friends who love and can eat it. Many innovative, thoughtful people are telephoning their invitations and asking guests, "Is there anything you can't eat?" It's best not to use the word allergy since most guests are reluctant to be the first to mention they have one. Then plan accordingly.

**Q.** *I am allergic to fresh flowers. The artificial ones I always used are now considered to be in poor taste. What do you recommend as a centerpiece for future dinner parties?*

**A.** Use an arrangement of silk, dried, or wood-fibre flowers. Glass or metal flowers make lovely fashionable centerpieces. Also consider statues or ornaments. A pretty soup tureen with candles on each side is a classic. Look around your house and use your imagination. The home decorating magazines show dozens of creative centerpieces that do not use fresh flowers.

# Beverages at Table

## Wine

**Q.** *How should one hold a stemmed wine glass?*

**A.** If it's chilled wine, hold the glass by the stem. Otherwise, hold the glass by the bowl. Each country has its own method.

In Germany the glass is held with the stem between the first and second fingers under the bowl. In Italy the glass is held by the bowl. In France the glass is held by the base of the glass, thumb on the top with the other fingers securing the bottom.

Q. *I know wine should be poured after the guests are seated, but my husband doesn't like to get up and go around the table filling glasses like a waiter. Is there an acceptable and attractive alternative?*

A. Yes. Here are two methods that work smoothly and they are attractive, and acceptable. Try both to determine which best suits your style.

(A) Place a bottle of wine at each end of the table in front of the host's and hostess' place setting. This is passed to your right and your husband's right for each guest to pour as much as he wants. This can be repeated as many times as you and your husband feel is necessary.

(B) You can place individual decanters which hold about two glasses of wine at each place setting. These decanters come in plain open top styles or a grape cluster style with stopper. Both are inexpensive and are sold at department stores and discount china outlets.

Q. *When my husband pours wine he fills the glasses. I want to discuss this with him but I'm not sure how much should be poured. What is the correct amount?*

A. No more than two-thirds full. For the large bubble glass, about one-half full. Some hosts and hostesses trying to be generous fill them to the brim and spilling is the usual result.

**Q.** *If I do not want wine, how do I let my host know without hurting his feelings?*

**A.** Allow him to pour you some wine. You need not drink it. It's good to have a glass to raise if someone offers a toast.

**Q.** *Could you give me a simple guide for the temperature of wines at serving time?*

**A.** The experts tell me the following. White wine and rosé should be chilled for two hours in a refrigerator or twenty minutes in a bucket filled with ice. If white wine is not cool enough, much of its appeal is lost. White wine that is too cold will have very little taste. Red wines taste best at cool room temperature, but it should not taste warm on your tongue. This would be equivalent to a cellar temperature.

**Q.** *My husband and I have just joined a "gourmet group" that dines in quality restaurants. Our first outing featured a six-course dinner with a wine for each course. Much to our surprise, a wine was served with the salad course (vinaigrette dressing), which I always thought was a no-no. Who is wrong, the restaurant or us?*

**A.** The restaurant is wrong. The only beverage that should be served with a green salad course or any salad with an acid dressing is a glass of chilled water.

## Toasts

**Q.** *Do women stand when a toast is given at official luncheons and dinners?*

**A.** If the toastmaster stands, all stand except the person receiving the toast. If the toastmaster remains seated, then all remain seated.

**Q.** *Can anyone offer a toast at a small private informal dinner party? Does the person offering the toast stand? How about the others?*

**A.** Yes; however, wait a few minutes and see if the host offers a toast after the first wine has been poured. Afterwards, a toast may be proposed by anyone present. It's best to remain seated when proposing a toast at a private informal dinner party. With space at a premium in most homes, getting up and sitting down can be disastrous.

**Q.** *When offering a toast, what is the purpose of touching glasses?*

**A.** In olden times, people clicked glasses in order that some of their drink would spill into each other's glass to assure that they were not being poisoned. Totally unnecessary today, but it's still done.

## Water

**Q.** *Should water be poured before or after the guests sit down to dinner?*

**A.** Water is poured to about one inch from the top of the glass before the guests sit down. Incidentally, the water should be chilled but do not put ice in the glass.

**Q.** *I always serve iced water with our meals. There is always a puddle of water around the glass that drips when the glass is lifted. Is there some way to prevent this?*

**A.** Water served at the table should be chilled but do not put ice in the glass. Ice is the culprit which causes condensation, hence, the puddle of water on your table.

Dorothea Johnson

## *Iced tea*

**Q.** *Many of us drink iced tea with our meals in the summertime, but by the time the meal is over there is a puddle of water on the table from the dripping glass. Do you have a solution?*

**A.** Yes, and it's a simple one. When you serve iced tea or any iced beverage at the table, place the glass on a small plate such as a bread and butter plate or a saucer to catch the drips and to hold the wet spoon. Any flatware once used should never be put back on the table or mat.

**Q.** *May I serve iced tea in my crystal water goblets for a Sunday dinner?*

**A.** Yes. Traditional rules for using crystal, china, and flatware need no longer apply. In today's home, personal expression is the only rule.

Dorothea Johnson

# *American and Continental Styles of Eating*

More and more Americans are turning to the continental style and no longer switch or zigzag their forks, but this is not the most popular way in America. There is no need to apologize for the style in which you eat. The important thing is to manipulate your knife and fork with assurance and ease. We acknowledge the continental style of eating just as the American method is accepted worldwide. Here are the basic differences and the correct ways to use each style.

## *American Style*

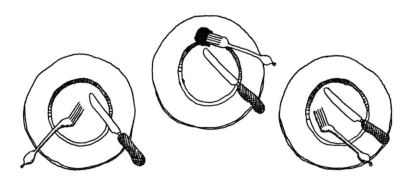

The knife is used only for cutting and is then placed on the side of the plate with the blade toward the center of the plate. The fork is then switched to the right hand and the food is conveyed to the mouth with the tines up. It is easier to eat the meat from your fork while it is still in the left hand, rather than turning the fork over and switching it to your right hand. Vegetables and other foods which do not require cutting are eaten with the fork in the right hand, tines up.

## Continental Style

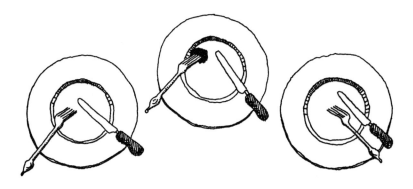

The continental style is more graceful and easier. You convey all food to the mouth with the fork in the left hand, knife in the right. Meat, potatoes and vegetables are eaten with the tines down. However, creamed foods, or slippery foods such as peas, are eaten with the tines up.

Dorothea Johnson

# *Setting the Table*

Place the flat silver in the order of its use. Use the piece on the outside first.

*Key:*

(1) Soup,
(2) Main course knife and fork,
(3) Salad knife and fork,
(4) Dessert fork and spoon.

# *Spooning and Drinking Soup*

Soup is spooned away from you toward the center of the bowl and sipped from the side of the spoon. If served in a soup plate, plate may be tipped slightly away from you to collect the last spoonfuls. If soup is served in a bowl with handles, or any cup with a handle, it may be picked up to drink the contents. Do not swirl soup or blow it to cool. Do not scrape the bottom of the bowl.

Soup may be served in regular teacups as a first course away from the dining table. For very rich soups, a demitasse cup or pot de creme works very well. Use the same spoon you would for demitasse.

Dorothea Johnson

# Knife and Fork Positions

Luncheon or dinner knives or forks are held this way

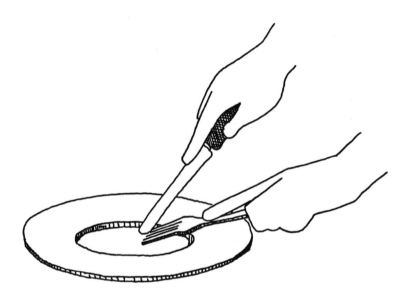

Do not place the knife and fork in this position.

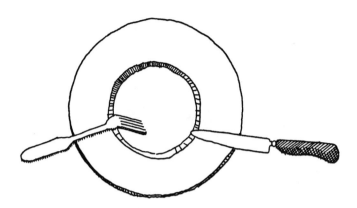

This is the only "rest" position. The knife and fork are crossed on the plate with the fork over the knife with the tines down.

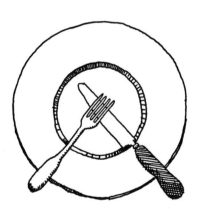

This is the "I am finished" position. The fork and knife are placed side by side with the blade of the knife facing the fork. Fork tines may be up or down. Both are acceptable.

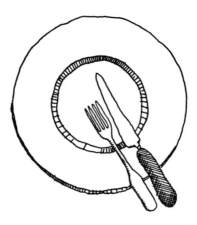

This is the "I am finished" position when eating only with the fork. Tines up.

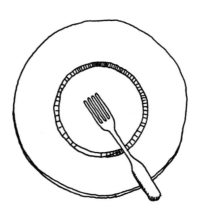

# Finger Bowls

The dessert plate can be served with the finger bowl, spoon and fork on the plate.

Remove the finger bowl and doily and place it on the table to the upper left of your plate. Then remove the fork to the left and the spoon to the right.

# *Eating Various Foods*

Some foods can be bothersome to eat, especially in public. Here are the accepted techniques for eating specific foods.

Artichokes (whole) are eaten with the fingers. Each leaf is removed separately, the soft end dipped in sauce and pulled through the teeth to remove the edible portion. Discard the remainder of the leaf on the side of the plate. The thistle is scraped away with a knife and fork. The heart is then cut into pieces and eaten with a fork.

Asparagus is cut into portions and eaten with a fork. In Europe it is eaten with the fingers.

Bacon is eaten with a knife and fork. Only very crisp bacon may be eaten with the fingers.

Bones from small birds such as quail, squab (and frog legs) may be held in one hand and brought to the mouth to be eaten without gnawing.

Bread. Break off one portion of your bread or roll at a time, then butter and eat it. Do the buttering on the plate, not in the hand.

Butter. When butter is passed, take your portion onto the butter plate with the butter knife. If pats are used, pick them up with a fork and place on your plate.

**Cake.** If served in small portions and non-sticky, it may be eaten with your fingers. Otherwise use a fork. If served with ice cream, use a fork and spoon.

**Celery, olives, pickles, and relishes** are taken from the serving tray with the fingers and placed on the side of your dinner plate or bread and butter plate. Celery and radishes can be dipped in salt and eaten with the fingers. Large olives with a stone are eaten in several bites, putting the pit on the side of the plate. Small stuffed olives are put in the mouth whole.

**Caviar.** Spread it on toast with a knife and eat with your fingers.

**Chicken, duck and turkey** are eaten with a knife and fork. Only at picnics is chicken eaten with the fingers.

**Clams** (steamed) are held by the shell in one hand and lifted out by the neck with the other hand. Slip off the inedible neck sheath with the fingers. Then the whole clam may be dipped in butter or broth and eaten in one bite.

**Clams** (fried) are eaten with a fork.

**Corn on the cob** is served only at casual meals. Butter and season several rows at a time, not the whole ear at once. Hold the ear firmly with fingers of both hands.

**Doughnuts.** Do not dunk in public. If the setting is casual, at home, and dunking makes the doughnut or toast taste better, go ahead.

**Eggs.** Hard-cooked eggs are eaten with a fork. Soft-cooked eggs served in an egg cup are eaten directly from the shell with a spoon. Slice off the cap with a knife. Soft-cooked eggs may also be scooped out of the shell and placed in a small dish and eaten with a spoon.

**Fish.** When served whole, slice off head, slit along backbone and remove top filet. Lift out the backbone, use the fork to slide the backbone out. If a few bones have remained, remove them from your mouth with thumb and forefinger and place them on the edge of your dinner plate or butter plate.

**Fruit**

*Apricots,* cherries, kumquats and plums (raw) are eaten with the fingers usually in one or two bites. The stones are dropped into the cupped hand and put on the side of the plate.

*Avocados* are eaten with a spoon when left in their shells. Otherwise pieces are eaten with a fork.

*Bananas* eaten at the table are peeled, broken into small pieces and eaten with the fingers. If away from the table, peel the banana down as you eat it.

*Berries* are eaten with a spoon. Large strawberries served with the stem are held by the stem, dipped in sugar, eaten in one or two bites, discarding the stem on the side of the plate.

*Fruit in a cocktail.* If fruit is on a toothpick you may eat it and discard the toothpick in an ashtray. In a tall glass, if the fruit is not on a toothpick it may be too messy to fuss with.

*Grapefruit* halves are served with sections loosened and eaten with a spoon. Do not attempt to squeeze out the juice except in the privacy of your own home.

*Grapes* are eaten by cutting a small portion away from the large bunch with a knife or scissors, then eaten one at a time. Seeds and inedible skins are removed from the mouth into cupped hand and placed on the side of the plate.

*Lemons.* When a wedge of lemon is served as a garnish for food, pick it up and press with your fingers. You may also pick it up with a fork and press out the juice with the other hand. If a slice of lemon is served, hold the slice with the fork and press out the juice with a knife.

*Mangoes* are cut in half, pit removed, then quartered. Place each quarter upside down and pull skin away while holding fruit with a fork. Cut into manageable pieces to eat with a fork.

*Oranges* are peeled with a sharp knife, then eaten section by section. If pre-sliced and served on a plate, the orange is then eaten with a fork.

*Peaches* are cut in half, then quartered. Pull the skin away from each quarter and eat with a fork.

*Pineapple* is eaten with a fork when served in quarters or slices. It is eaten with a spoon when served cut up.

*Stewed fruits* are eaten with a spoon. Pits are dropped into the spoon and placed on the side of the plate.

*Watermelon* is eaten with a fork unless cubed. Then it is eaten with a spoon. Seeds are dropped into cupped hand and placed on the side of the plate.

**Ice cream.** Today, ice cream is most often served in a sherbet dish and is eaten with a small spoon. There is no practical basis for both a fork and spoon unless the ice cream is served on a dessert plate with cake. If both implements are provided, use the fork for the solid part of the ice cream, the spoon for the softer part. When served as Baked Alaska, it is eaten with a fork and spoon. The fork is held in the left hand to guide the portion onto the spoon.

**Lobsters** are difficult to eat. The claws are cracked with a nutcracker. The meat is extracted with a seafood fork, dipped in butter or sauce, and eaten. Large pieces are first cut with a fork. The delicacies of tamale (green) and roe (coral) are eaten with a fork. The small claws are pulled off and cleaned, drawing as through a straw. Stuffed lobster is eaten with a knife and fork. Hard-shelled crabs are eaten the same way.

**Fresh oysters, mussels and clams.** Use an oyster fork for oysters, mussels and clams served on the half-shell. Hold the shell with the one hand and remove the oyster, mussel or clam whole with the fork. Dip it in the sauce and eat it in one mouthful. Mussels served on toothpicks may be eaten directly from the toothpick. If served in a sauce, use an oyster fork to remove them from their shells. You also may pick up a mussel in your fingers and suck mussel and sauce from the shell.

**Pâté de Foie Gras.** Put on toast or crackers with a knife and eat with the fingers.

**Potatoes.** Baked are eaten from the skin with a fork. The skin may be eaten with a knife and fork. Butter is added by taking butter from your butter plate with the dinner fork. Do not mash any kind of potato on your plate. Chips are eaten with the fingers. Shoestring potatoes are eaten with the fingers. French fries are halved and eaten with a fork.

**Relishes,** jellies, conserves, cranberry sauce, or horseradish should be put on the dinner plate.

**Salad** is eaten with a fork. Wedges and large sections may be cut with a knife. Salad served as a separate course is eaten with the salad knife and fork. If you feel you can manage without the knife, it may be left on the table. Often there is no knife for the salad.

**Salt** should be placed on the edge of the dinner plate if used for dipping. If open salts do not have salt spoons, take salt with the tip of a clean knife or use your thumb and forefinger. Do not dip any foods into salt trays.

**Sandwiches.** Tea types and canapes are eaten with the fingers. Club sandwiches may be eaten with a knife and fork or cut into fourths and eaten with the fingers. Open-faced sandwiches are eaten with a knife and fork.

**Sauces** may be poured over meat or beside meat with a forkful of food at a time dipped into the sauce.

**Shrimp cocktail** is eaten with a seafood fork. Eat large shrimp in two bites or if possible, place on serving plate and cut with fork.

**Shrimp** with tails left on may be held by the tail with fingers, dipped in sauce, bitten off, and tail discarded.

**Snails.** If tongs are provided hold shell with tongs and pull out snail with oyster fork. Otherwise hold shell with fingers. The snail is eaten whole. Bread may be dipped in the garlic butter.

**Soft-shelled crabs** are cut with a knife and eaten with a fork.

**Soup** is spooned away from you toward center of bowl and sipped from the side of the spoon. If served in a soup plate, plate may be tipped slightly away from you to collect the last spoonfuls. If soup is served in a bowl with handles, or any cup with a handle, it may be picked up to drink the contents. Do not swirl soup or blow it to cool. Do not scrape bottom of the bowl.

**Spaghetti** may be twirled with a fork and spoon, or a fork alone. It is best to twirl a few strands with a fork alone. Do not stir spaghetti. Even in Italy there is no fixed rule about this.

**Tortillas.** Place flat in hand or plate. Fill, roll up. Eat from the end.

**Water.** Blot mouth before taking a drink. Do not drink water while food is in the mouth, or roll water around mouth, or swallow loudly. If you've taken too hot a mouthful of food, sip a bit of water. Do not forcefully drain an entire glassful. Hold a tumbler type glass near the bottom, a small stem glass by the stem and large goblets at the bottom of the bowl.

# Easy Entertaining

Buffet Suppers
Invitations
Alternative Buffet Table Settings
Setting and Decorating the Buffet Table
Serving the Buffet Supper
The Seated Buffet Supper
Serving the Wine at Buffet Suppers
Serving the Dessert and Coffee at a Traditional Buffet Supper
Serving the Dessert and Coffee at a Seated Buffet Supper
Menu
Food for Buffet Suppers

Dorothea Johnson

# Buffet Suppers

Buffet meals served in the evening are called suppers. The word is pronounced boo-fay, not buff-fay. One should specify buffet brunch, luncheon, or supper.

Patterns of entertaining change and with the informal do-it-yourself attitude of today, the buffet supper is the easiest and most popular way to entertain friends with a minimum of space and help. There are two ways of seating guests at a buffet supper. One is the traditional buffet supper where guests serve themselves and sit any place that is available, balancing the plate on their lap. The other is the seated buffet supper at which guests serve themselves and sit at designated tables. As with any meal, the quality of the food and wines, the appearance of the table, and the presentation of the food will determine the tone of the party.

# Invitations

This method works best. Telephone your invitation. State clearly who you are, the type of party you are giving, the date, hour, and place. If your invitation is accepted, tell your guest if it's informal, black tie, or bring your swim suit. No surprises, please. Guests want to know just what you've planned so they will not be taken by surprise. About five days before your party send a reminder. For the newcomers send directions or a map. A hand sketched map can be mimeographed inexpensively. Your guests will be grateful and you will be happy to see them arrive on time.

Dorothea Johnson

# *Alternative Buffet Table Settings*

Plates
  Brown rice
    Veal Stroganoff
      Fresh broccoli
        Tossed Green Salad
          Bread
          (buttered)
            Silver
            (rolled in napkins)

Alternative Table Setting A

Alternative Table Setting B

If your group is exceptionally large, have a duplicate of each of the various dishes on opposite sides of the table and have your guests form two lines.

We are describing buffet suppers, traditional and seated, without help. With any type of entertaining you may choose to have help or do everything yourself. Naturally this is up to the host or hostess.

138

Dorothea Johnson

# Setting and Decorating the Buffet Table

The buffet table itself will be the center of attraction. A dining table is probably the most convenient and natural place to set up the supper. A rented long collapsible table works well, or a long table which might be no more than a sturdy door or a large piece of plyboard supported on trestles. The table can be set up in the corner or center of a room—any place that is convenient in your house and accessible to the kitchen as well as to the guests.

Your buffet table can be as simple or as elaborate as you choose. If your table top is a beautiful wood, leave it bare. Or cover any table to the floor with fabric. Sheets work beautifully and can be coordinated to fit your party decor and house.

Arrange dishes in natural sequence so that first things come first. It's confusing to find the rice placed after the stroganoff. (See Alternative Table Setting A.)

The traditional floral centerpiece is lovely; indeed, it is the most popular. But a centerpiece can be as imaginative as the host or hostess. Let your imagination soar. For today's centerpiece, anything goes. Try what's growing in the garden—vegetables or fruits that can be eaten after the party. Here are some centerpiece suggestions:

**Vegetables in season**—cabbage, carrots, turnips, rutabagas.

Striped squash, dried corn, gourds, or eggplant. Pile in a basket or silver bowl that has been strewn with autumn leaves. Stick a few leaves among the vegetables.

Fresh corn, tomatoes, peppers, and squash—add an eggplant to set the whole thing off.

Pineapple, pears, peaches, melons, apricots, grapes.

**Pots of chrysanthemums**—transfer from clay pots to ceramic pots, lined baskets, or silver bowls. After using them inside, plant them outside for further enjoyment.

*Spring*—buy flats of annuals such as marigolds. Cover a basket with leaves and set the plants in or transfer them to ceramic dishes. Later plant them outside to be enjoyed until the first frost.

Surround a large pineapple with a lei of small apples, lemons or pears to accent a *Hawaiian supper.*

Tulips are perfect for *Easter*—turn back some of the petals to give them an airy look.

White carnations and limes—a cool note for a *summer supper.* Arrange the carnations in a large pedestal-type dish. Place on a silver, ceramic, or wicker plate and pile in the limes

*Oriental supper*—accent a graceful piece of driftwood with several bright blossoms in small individual vases.

*Seafood supper*—pile seashells in a wicker basket, silver or ceramic bowl.

*Italian supper*—use a straw basket, wooden or silver bowl. Fill with cans of Italian tomatoes, paste, and sauce. Stick in some pepperoni sausage and waxed provolone cheese.

# Serving the Buffet Supper

When all the food has been set out, supper is announced by the host or hostess. Ask a woman guest, usually the wife of the guest of honor, or the eldest or most distinguished woman present, to start the buffet service. The hostess should go directly to the buffet table to direct traffic and help the guests. Since most of the dishes can be handled with a spoon alone, a good place for the hostess to help is with the salad. Meanwhile, the host can be giving his attention to the wine. The host and hostess serve themselves last. When the guests have finished, tell them what to do with their plates or remove them yourself. A large wicker tray can be very helpful for a temporary depository and for removal of used plates.

Dorothea Johnson

# The Seated Buffet Supper

The supper can be set out on a sideboard or on the dining table as described in *Setting and Decorating the Buffet Table*. If it's set on a sideboard, seating can be at the dining table or at several smaller tables. Space would determine how many tables you could have. The best seating plan is for you to install yourself at one table and your spouse at another. If you have more than two tables, ask friends to be the host or hostess at each table. If one table has to be placed far away from the rest of the party, make sure you or your husband sit at this table. There is honor in being seated with the host or hostess, even if he or she is out in the left field. Guests help themselves and sit at designated tables. Place cards are helpful for guests and the hosts. Again the host and hostess serve themselves last.

*A Seated
Buffet Supper
Table Setting*

The table may be set as usual, but since this is an informal party, there are no rules. If you own place plates, I opt for putting them on the table when it's set up and leaving them there throughout the meal. Most of us live in a servantless world and the antiquated custom of removing the place plate makes little sense today. Place plates can be used for any type of meal and they keep the table looking attractive and tidy throughout the meal. If one doesn't own place plates, just picture the table setting minus the plates.

Guests serve themselves at the buffet table, then take their seats at the table, placing the dinner plate on the place plate. When they have finished eating, they remove the dinner plate *only,* replacing it with a dessert plate.

# Serving The Wine At Buffet Suppers

For a traditional buffet supper, it's best not to place glasses of wine on the buffet table. It's difficult for a guest to handle a plate of food, silver, napkin, and a glass of wine while trying to find a place to sit. Especially if that place happens to be the floor. Here are two methods that work well. Determine which best suits your style.

(A) Place glasses and bottles or carafes of wine in key spots wherever guests will be sitting. Ask guests to help themselves or ask a friend to be in charge of pouring the wine.

(B) The host fills the wine glasses (no more than one-half full) and passes them on a tray. He can refill glasses or leave bottles or carafes of wine in key spots, asking a friend to be in charge of refilling glasses.

For a seated buffet supper, put one or more bottles or carafes of wine on each table and let guests pour their own or ask a man at each table to be in charge of the wine.

# Serving the Dessert and Coffee at a Traditional Buffet Supper

Here are four methods for serving dessert and coffee. The number of guests at your supper would determine which method best suits your style.

(A) Dessert and coffee can be set up on a separate table or sideboard. Guests can help themselves. Host or hostess stands by to help.

(B) The buffet table can be cleared and dessert and coffee placed on it for guests to help themselves. Host or hostess stands by to help.

(C) The host and hostess can personally serve each guest dessert and coffee from a teacart, table or sideboard.

(D) A platter or pedestal dish of finger-type desserts (tarts, lemon bars, brandy balls) can be passed along with small dessert plates. The hostess can then serve coffee.

# Serving the Dessert and Coffee at a Seated Buffet Supper

Keep in mind the number of guests you will be accommodating at your supper and your available space. You may use the same methods listed for a traditional buffet or consider one of the following.

(A) If space permits, tell your guests that dessert and coffee will be served in the living room. You can manage easily from a teacart or table set up for this purpose.

(B) A centerpiece of fresh fruit can be used for dessert. This could be a bowl of strawberries. Dessert plates and cream could be put on the table and guests could help themselves. Coffee could be served later by the host or hostess in the living room or, if the hostess prefers, at table. I find it easier to leave the table and serve coffee elsewhere.

# *Menu*

A menu may be put on the table for any meal no matter how formal, informal or casual. A handwritten menu placed between the plates and the main course can be a charming addition to a buffet table. It also stimulates conversation. One may use an old-fashioned china stand which can be written on with a thin-tipped magic marker, then washed and used over and over. Or a plain white menu card, a handmade decorated pasteboard card or any of the attractive and colorful message cards sold in stationery departments may be used. For casual entertaining, I have written menus on paper lunch sacks.

For a buffet supper the menu card should be held in a stand so that it can be easily read by guests. A small picture easel makes a good menu stand.

For a seated buffet supper, you can put one menu card on the buffet table and one or two at each table where guests will be seated. For the latter, use stands or lay them flat on the table.

Two sample menu cards appear on the following pages.

Menu

Chicken Curry

Rice

Condiments

Assorted Chutneys

Beer

Orange Spoom

or

Fresh Fruits Grand Marnier

Madeleines

Coffee

Menu

Beef and Vodka Casserole

Bulgur Wheat

Fresh Broccoli

Tossed Green Salad

Hearty Burgundy
or
Chenin Blanc Wine

Minted Pears
or
Frozen Lemon Soufflé

Coffee

# Food for Buffet Suppers

Today no one wants to be stuffed with food. You don't have to offer an extensive menu to entertain successfully. Don't pull out all the stops and offer every specialty of the house. A beef or fowl main course dish, bulgur wheat, a vegetable, salad, dessert and coffee make up a fine menu. For traditional buffet suppers, feature foods that do not require the use of a knife. A dish such as Chicken Gumbo is good. Do not serve a meat dish with bones at a buffet supper.

For a seated buffet supper, serve any foods normally offered at a seated meal.

# Military Etiquette

**Q.** *At a social gathering, how do I introduce my husband who is Colonel Robert Jones?*

**A.** Introduce him as *my husband Bob Jones.* If people know your last name, all you need say is *Bob, my husband.* Call him *Bob* when talking to other officers and their wives, even though they may be younger. To employees, waiters, young children, etc., refer to him as *Colonel Jones.*

**Q.** *How are chaplains and doctors introduced in the military?*

**A.** Chaplains are introduced as Chaplain, doctors by their rank.

**Q.** *How do I introduce Colonel Smith and Major Jones?*

**A.** The person of higher rank is always mentioned first. For example: Colonel Smith, Major Jones. Never use the third person when speaking *to* or *of an officer.* There are many officers with the same rank. Do not say, *Does the Colonel care for a drink?* Say instead, *Colonel Smith, would you like a drink?*

**Q.** *Can a Lieutenant Colonel's rank be shortened to Colonel for introductions?*

**A.** No. Introduce him as Lieutenant Colonel Smith. The reply should be, *How do you do, Colonel Smith?*

**Q.** *When at a dinner party given by and for military officers and their wives, who leaves first?*

**A.** The senior officer leaves first, then others may follow.

**Q.** *How do I correctly address an envelope to Lieutenant Commander and Mrs. John Wheelwright? Can I abbreviate his rank?*

**A.** No. An officer's rank is never abbreviated in a social address. Two examples are listed below. Both are correct.

Lieutenant Commander and Mrs. John Wheelwright
Street address
City, State, and zip code

Lieutenant Commander John Wheelwright
and Mrs. Wheelwright
Street address
City, State, and zip code

When addressing an envelope, one should *never* use the following: Lieutenant Commander and Mrs. John Wheelwright, USN. USN should *only* be used after the name of the person who is in the Navy. The wife of a military man is *not* in his branch of service. The following is correct.

Lieutenant Commander John Wheelwright, USN
and Mrs. Wheelwright
Street address
City, State, and zip code

**Q.** *How do I address an invitation to Colonel Mary Smith who is married to Adam Jones?*

**A.** Colonel Mary Smith and Mr. Adam Jones
      or
Colonel Mary Smith
and Mr. Adam Jones
Street address
City, State, and zip code

**Q.** *We attended a party recently and heard a Marine Corps officer referred to as a "Full Colonel." Is there such a rank?*

**A.** No. There is no such rank in the Marine Corps or any other branch of the military service. An officer is either a Lieutenant Colonel or a Colonel. I am aware of the common usage of the term, "Full Colonel," however, the fact that one hears "Full Colonel," "Bird Colonel," and "Light Colonel," frequently does not make it correct nor should its incorrect usage be confused as a custom, courtesy, or tradition.

**Q.** *I have been married for three weeks to a military officer. We were walking down the street and I asked him to carry my umbrella which he refused to do. His only excuse was that he wasn't supposed to. Why?*

**A.** An officer wearing his uniform does not carry an umbrella. It's simply not part of the uniform.

# Party Record

A Party Record can be an invaluable
resource to a host or hostess. Not only does it
serve as a reminder of how you entertained
certain people the last time, but it contains
all the elements of *that* successful party.
Sample and blank forms are provided to start
you on your permanent record.

Dorothea Johnson

# *Sample Party Record*

| | |
|---|---|
| **Date, time** | Friday, November 20, 19___ at 7:00 o'clock |
| **Type of party** | Buffet supper (seated) |
| **Occasion** | Farewell party for Helen and Bob Jones |
| **Dress** | Informal (Men—business suits, Women—evening dresses) Les, grey pin-stripe suit; I will wear a black midi-length evening dress |

## *Menu*

Raw Vegetables
Yogurt Dip

Breast of Chicken Wellington
Mushroom Sauce

Bulgur Wheat Pilaf

Romaine Lettuce
and
Hearts of Palm Salad

Cheese

Pinot Chardonnay Wine

Frozen Lemon Soufflé
Raspberry Sauce

Madeleine

Coffe

### Guest List and Drink Preference

2 Helen and Bob Jones (White wine)
2 Alice and Bill Smith (Perrier—scotch)
2 Regina and Ned Diehl (White wine—vodka)
2 Jean and Walt Scribes (White wine)
2 Jan and Pete Day (?)
1 Liz Coleman (?)
1 John Elkins (?)
2 Regina and Ned Worth (Vodka and Perrier)
2 Us
—
16 Total Number of Guests

159

Dorothea Johnson

# *Table Setting and Decoration*

Dark blue and white china plates. Copper place plates. White linen napkins, each tied with a dark blue grosgrain ribbon to which a place card has been attached.

Buffet supper served from dining table. Two round tables, each seating eight, set up in living room. Tables skirted to floor with dark blue sheeting. One large menu on buffet table and two small ones on each round table. Centerpiece of metal bachelor's buttons (dark blue) in glass bowls flanked by numerous dark blue votive candles in glass containers on two round tables.

Two carafes of wine on each round table.

## *Cost*

food                                    _____

liquors                                 _____

wine                                    _____

potted marigolds                        _____

miscellaneous expenses                  _____

Total cost

Dorothea Johnson

# *Party Record*

Date, time

Type of party

Occasion

Dress

## *Menu*

## *Guest List*

Dorothea Johnson

# *Table Setting and Decoration*

## Cost

food .................................... ———

liquors .................................. ———

wine .................................... ———

flowers ................................. ———

miscellaneous expenses ................... ———

Total Cost                                ———

# *Party Record*

Date, time

Type of party

Occasion

Dress

## *Menu*

## *Guest List*

Dorothea Johnson

## *Table Setting and Decoration*

## *Cost*

food . . . . . . . . . . . . . . . . . . . . . . . . . . . . . . . . . . . . . . . . . .  _____

liquors . . . . . . . . . . . . . . . . . . . . . . . . . . . . . . . . . . . . . . . .  _____

wine  . . . . . . . . . . . . . . . . . . . . . . . . . . . . . . . . . . . . . . . . .  _____

flowers  . . . . . . . . . . . . . . . . . . . . . . . . . . . . . . . . . . . . . . .  _____

miscellaneous expenses  . . . . . . . . . . . . . . . . . . . . . . .  _____

Total Cost

Dorothea Johnson

# *Party Record*

Date, time

Type of party

Occasion

Dress

## *Menu*

## *Guest List*

165

Dorothea Johnson

# *Table Setting and Decoration*

,

## *Cost*

food .................................... ———

liquors ................................. ———

wine ................................... ———

flowers ................................. ———

miscellaneous expenses .................... ———

**Total Cost**

# Index